ASK ANNE & NAN

ASK

ANNE & NAN

WHETSTONE PUBLISHING

Brattleboro, Vermont 05301

*To our dear readers,
and to our children—
Fred and Avery;
Lucinda, Suzanne and Philip—
without whose patience,
forbearance and occasional
bursts of derision this book could
never have been possible. And a
special thank you from Nancy
to her husband, Rich.*

CONTENTS

PREFACE

A year ago this month—December 13, 1987, to be exact—I was enjoying a leisurely cup of coffee over the Vermont Living section of the *Rutland Herald* when my wife said, "Hey, Anne and Nan are looking for a publisher."

I had been a fan of the authors' helpful how-to-do-it column for several years, and a publisher of books and a periodical on bicycle racing for several more. That Sunday I gave the notion of publishing a book of Anne and Nan's advice scant thought. But over the next week the idea grew on me, and I set a date to meet with them in my Brattleboro office on December 30.

On that cold, but brilliantly sunny winter day we shared coffee thick as sludge, groused about Vermont winters and began the process that led to the book you hold in your hands.

It has been fun, in part because of the variety (sometimes to the point of oddity) and humor in the 300-plus letters and responses between these covers. But more, perhaps, because Anne and Nan offer not only down-to-earth advice, but a glimpse into a way of life where there's often more time than money, where old things have value and solutions to problems don't always come in packages.

Dan Woodbury
Whetstone Publishing
December 1988

ABOUT THE AUTHORS

The meeting of Anne and Nan, summer 1982, Skunk Hollow Tavern, Hartland Four Corners, Vermont:

Brought together by a mutual friend, we discovered that what we had in common went beyond our flypaper minds. We had both lived in Cambridge, Massachusetts, and in suburbs of Detroit, albeit different ones. We had each moved to Vermont more than 20 years ago. We both had been divorced, although Nan had remarried. We both had been single parents. We both had worked in the private and nonprofit sector. Most importantly, we are both inquisitive and we *love* mail.

We like many of the same books and music and we are the only people we know of our age who subscribe to *Rolling Stone*. We like gardening, anything that flickers, coffee thick as sludge and asking questions.

Anne is enormously envious of Nan's chickens, especially of Buck-Buck, the classy Polish Buff rooster who thinks he's a dog. Anne's envy of Nan's greenhouse was so great that she copied it. Nan is envious of Anne's 18th century farmhouse nestled on a chunk of land that is well protected from developers.

Our differences are few but deep. Nan is a compulsive fitness addict. Anne, on the other hand, thinks exercise was invented by the devil. Nan prefers watching videotapes in the evening, while Anne likes hers at 5 a.m. Anne is devoted to cats and dogs. Nan is devoted to dogs and chickens.

Anne works as a freelance writer and is also the director of The Woodstock Learning Clinic, which operates two nonprofit centers for preschool children with special needs. Nan began working as a stringer for the *Rutland Daily Herald* in 1973 and went on to start a weekly newspaper. She now works as a freelance writer and is involved in advocacy for learning-disabled children and land preservation.

ACKNOWLEDGMENTS

We couldn't write our column without help from our friends. The people listed below are ones we have called on time and again. They have been saintlike in their patience with us as well as unfailingly helpful, often doing investigative footwork on our behalf way beyond the reasonable call of duty. To those we have listed, our thanks. To those we have inadvertently omitted, our apologies.

Dr. James Roberts, DVM, and his assistant, Sue Bradley, of the Woodstock Veterinary Clinic, Woodstock

Norm Patch of Ascutney Antiques in Ascutney

Pat Baril, of Barre, our cooking expert

Sanford Stele, our New York City-based intrepid investigator

K. Daryle Thomas, The Hearth and Cricket Shop, East Wallingford, who answers our questions about woodstoves, fireplaces and all things relating to the above

All the good folks at the Norman Williams Public Library, Woodstock

Jonathan Schechtman of Meeting House Furniture Restoration, Quechee

Everyone at the UVM Extension Service

Barney Bloom of the Vermont Historical Society, Montpelier

Earl Thomsen, of Brandon—repairer, restorer and historian of all things caned, wickered, fibered, rushed and splinted

Meredith Wright, of Montpelier—expert on fabric restoration and conservation

Richard Adelson, Antiquarian Bookseller, Pomfret

Frank Teagle, citizen extraordinaire, Woodstock

Charles Fenton, Woodstock Gallery, Woodstock

Bill Borger and his wife Louise of Authorized Applicance Service in Rutland

B.G.'s Market, Hartland Three Corners

Tom Fagan, Charles Tuttle Antiquarian Books in Rutland

The unfailingly helpful folks at F. H. Gillingham and Sons, Woodstock, with a special thanks to Millie Bushnell and Jireh Billings

Dudley P. Whitney, McPerson extraordinaire and saver of all things lost on the Mac

Jim Fournier of Jim's Paints in Windsor

Bob Stacey of Stacey's TrueValue Hardware in Windsor

Gail Furnas, former head librarian, Windsor Public Library, who found authors of obscure poems and doggerel, with equal enthusiasm

Mary and Karen of Pegton's Yardstick in Burlington

John W. and John A. DeCook, of Claremont, New Hampshire—jewelers, watchmakers and restorers of antique watches, including those whose workings are eaten by puppies

Tanya Lipinski Wilkins, formerly with the Sullivan County Extension Service, who always seemed delighted with our questions and always found answers

The staff at the Sullivan County Extension Service

The staff of the Windsor Public Library

The staff of the Windsor Animal Hospital

Bob Hingston of C & S Sports in Windsor

Jon Soderstrom, fixer of all things great and small

Lee Tebbetts, for bringing us together

. . . and all the readers who have sent us letters, pamphlets, booklets, catalogues, clippings, copies, and, upon occasion, books that they thought might be helpful to us (and were).

FOREWORD

Do you know what to use to clean your mother's tombstone?

If not, read on. You need this book.

Here, disguised as a compendium of handy household hints, is a minor delight: a book of useful information that's also fun to read. Where else would you find out that the best way to have your refrigerator repainted is probably to take it to an auto body shop? Or where you can send your stuck-together stamp collection to be freeze-dried? (And thereby, presumably, unstuck.) Or the best method for preserving comic books?

Not only do the ever-resourceful authors offer the best formula for window cleaning and tell you how to get baked-on creosote out of an old chimney, they do it with wit and style. And they have the wit and style to know when to offer counsel, rather than advice. The second entry of their first chapter is a classic, and should be memorized by all the authors of all the dull homeowner-advice books ever printed: How do you clean gunk that can't be reached out from behind a stove that can't be moved? "You don't," declare Anne and Nan, with an economy of comment worthy of Calvin Coolidge.

The secret of this book (and the *Vermont Sunday Magazine* column from which it is compiled) is that there are no secrets. Unlike many purveyors of advice, Anne and Nan make no attempt to present themselves as oracles. They tell the reader their sources, and quite often describe the process they went through to find their answers. They invite reader comment and when it turns up a simpler, better solution they print that too.

Their obvious assumption—that all of us are smarter than any of us—is both wise and time-proven. If Anne and Nan don't have the answer, they'll know where to find it, and will share the information with the rest of us.

Tom Slayton
Editor
Vermont Life Magazine

ASK ANNE & NAN

CHAPTER 1

KITCHEN AND BATH CLEANING

We are not people whose idea of an amusing morning is cleaning the kitchen (or anything else, for that matter) and so we had to do a great deal of research to find the answers to the questions in this section. They have stood us in great stead, as we hope they will our readers. Without a doubt, our greatest discovery has been baking soda, which cleans almost everything, and dishwasher detergent, which cleans everything else. We have had two "recipes" that have been requested again and again. One is for our homemade window-washing mixture, and the other for our shower-curtain washing procedure.

GENERAL KITCHEN CLEAN-UP

Q: It's time for me to do something about my dirty kitchen. Everything is coated with grease and smoke residue. Given that state of things, I obviously spend as little time as possible cleaning and scrubbing. Is there a shortcut?

L. M. H., Hartland

A: What nylon net is to Heloise, dishwasher detergent is to us: ½ cup dissolved in 1 gallon of hot water will remove dirt, grease, grime and woodsmoke residue. It also works like magic on kerosene-lamp chimneys. They'll sparkle after a good soak; dry and polish with wadded sheets of newspaper.

Q: How do you clean gunk or layers of dust in back of a gas stove that can't be reached by a mop or broom and where the stove can't be moved in order to clean it? I can't reach in back by hand.

J. Hayward, Montpelier

A: You don't.

WOOD CABINETS

Q: How can we remove masking tape from wood cabinets?

Unsigned, Poultney

A: Weldwood Cleaner and Thinner is guaranteed to remove dried adhesive from wood, plastic, glass, laminates and fabric: it is available at hardware or paint stores. According to our neighbor, who told us about this wonderful product, it will also remove chewing gum from the above-mentioned surfaces. He used it to remove some well ground-in chewing gum from the knee of his trousers, and the gum came off clean as a whistle. We recommend, however, that you do a spot check first on rugs and fabrics to make absolutely sure the dye won't be affected.

Weldwood contains methylene chloride and petroleum distillate and is highly flammable. Please use with extreme caution.

Q: My kitchen cabinets are wood and about 22 years old. I've tried everything to clean them: Liquid Gold, furniture polish, etc. Murphy Oil Soap left the cabinets white. They don't look clean, and it's frustrating after spending an hour to have them look smudgy.

N. W., Barre

A: We think your cabinet problem is the result of years of wax and grease accumulation; the wax- and oil-based products you are using are only adding insult to injury. We suggest you take a paint thinner (*not* a stripper) and, pouring some on a clean cloth, rub your cabinets with the grain until all the build-up is gone. Finish the job by using Number 0004 steel wool: rub lightly, again with the grain, until you get a consistent sheen. Then apply Liquid Gold, lemon oil or whatever. Your smudge problem should be solved.

FORMICA

Q: The Formica top of my kitchen cabinets and around my sink got terribly stained after 17 years of use. After I had used several "scrubs," a friend suggested I use pure bleach, let it stand and rinse off. I did, and it worked so well it completely removed the finish. Now every little thing that touches the counter leaves a stain worse than before. I waxed it, and that's fine until water hits the counter, which is every day. I called the Formica people in Rutland who installed it, and they don't know what to do, short of replacing the counter top. Any suggestions on how to put back a finish and a shine?

Gloria Anderson, West Rutland

A: Tsk, tsk. Your Formica people should be ashamed of themselves. There is a product on the market made by Nybco, called Tough as Tile, which is an epoxy enamel. It can be used to provide a lasting, shiny finish on Formica, porcelain, enamel or any comparable surface that is subject to severe wear and frequent washing. It is 100-percent nontoxic, lead-free and baby-safe and comes in a wide variety of colors. Before you use it, make sure you have gotten all the old wax off the Formica or the epoxy enamel won't bond properly.

For future reference and for those of our readers who also suffer from stained Formica counters, there is a liquid called Sunnyside

Plastic Cleaner that cleans and polishes Formica, Plexiglas, Lucite, Acrylite and all other nonporous plastics. It works like a dream. Both Tough as Tile and Sunnyside are available in hardware stores.

FLOORS

Q: We hope you can help us with our kitchen floor. It is only three years old and has developed a yellowish tinge in two or three spots. (The basic color is off-white.) It can't be wax build-up as it is a no-wax floor and we've never used any of the commercial products that are sold these days for no-wax floors. Do you have any ideas as to what the yellowing might be and how we can get rid of it? We've tried several cleaning products, even bleach. The floor is Armstrong no-wax Sundial Solarium if that helps.

C. R., Rutland

A: We're afraid there is no hope for your floor. The absolutely worst thing you could have done was use bleach; the second-worst thing was to have used "several cleaning products." The use of both has spelled irredeemable disaster.

Although it won't get rid of the yellowish tinge, you might improve the look of the floor with an application of New Beginning, a product made by Armstrong specifically for cleaning and refinishing the surface of pretreated but worn linoleum. In the future, wash your floor with a mixture of clear water and white vinegar, rinse and let dry. Then apply a coat of Armstrong's Shine Keeper according to directions. Both these products are available from your Armstrong dealer. You can find the one closest to you in the Yellow Pages.

While researching your question we were interested to learn that asphalt, tracked in from a paved driveway, can discolor a no-wax floor, as can putting an area rug on its surface.

APPLIANCES

Q: I recently purchased a house that came with appliances. The refrigerator is covered with decals. How can they be removed without damaging the surface of the refrigerator?

Georgiana Eddy, East Wallingford

A: Paint the decals with several coats of white vinegar. Give the vinegar time to soak in and then wipe off.

READER FEEDBACK: Laurie Gauthice, of Fairlee, wrote: "There is a product for removing decals called Meyercord Decal Remover. The manufacturer's address is 365 E. North Ave., Carol Stream, IL 60188."

Q: I have been trying to find someone who will come to our home and paint our stove and refrigerator to match our kitchen. Can you help?

M. V., Montpelier

A: We are reluctant to recommend that you have this kind of work done in your home as the type of paint used (despite claims to the contrary) will not stand up to the wear and tear of everyday household use. If you want a super job that will last, you should have an automobile body shop do the work. They will paint your appliances with the same lacquer-based, spray-on paint that is used on cars. We suggest you call two or three body shops in your area and get an estimate: include pick-up and delivery. You'll be inconvenienced for three or four days, but it will be worth it.

Q: I'm tired of doing almost the same amount of work to keep up a frost-free refrigerator while paying a lot extra on my electricity bill. I find I have to turn off the fridge two or three times a year to clean it anyway, and defrosting would take only a little more time and effort. Can I have the frost-free mechanisms (fan, heating coils or whatever) disconnected, leaving me with a non-frost-free refrigerator that would be cheaper to run?

G., Bethel

A: We called the General Electric Answer Center (800-626-2000). We have found them to be a polite and helpful resource when we've had questions on electric appliances, whether G.E. or any other brand. They said they get many calls from people complaining that their electric bills have soared since they purchased a frost-free refrigerator, but the facts just don't bear this out. (G.E. said, "It's really a psychological, rather than an actual problem.") First, the compressors in the new frost-free refrigerators are more energy-efficient than the old ones. Although they run more, they pull less wattage overall. In addition the new fridges are better insulated. You can figure a frost-free will cost about $8 a month to run, while a new, energy-efficient manual-defrost model will cost about $5.50. It's hard to believe that the wattage used by your old fridge was as low as for a brand new one, but even if it was, you are paying, at the most, about $3 more per month for electricity.

G.E. strongly advises against tampering with any appliance's innards. Your fridge was designed and built as a frost-free model, and the operation of certain components depends upon the presence of others. Dissection can only mean disaster down the road, and it's highly unlikely that a responsible appliance-repair person would be willing to take the risks involved in making any modifications.

Q: I'm a lousy housekeeper, and my microwave oven is a disaster. Is there an easy way to clean it?

L. N. D., Chester

A: There is indeed. Take a one-quart Pyrex dish and fill it half full of water. Put it in your microwave on High for about five minutes. Wipe out the oven, put clean water in the dish and give it another five minutes on High. Be sure to wipe around the door and gasket.

Q: I have a KitchenAid dishwasher, Model Imperial 21, which is only two years old. I use Cascade for a detergent. In the past six months my glasses have come out cloudy and etched and the dishes feel as if they aren't rinsed properly. We do have a water softener for our water system. According to our manual, etching is due to mineral deposits. However, for over 1 1/2 years I never had this problem and I had previously washed good crystal, etc., in the same machine. It is now ruining all my glassware. You cannot remove the deposits from the glass. I've checked all the arms and wands, and everything seems to be working fine. What's wrong?

Marlene Velander, Montpelier

A: The consensus among the plumber and the KitchenAid people we spoke with is that the problem is almost certainly in your water softener. Frequently the softener will seem to be working (i.e., it is using up the salt in the barrel) when in fact it is not backwashing properly. We suggest you have someone come and look at it or, if you prefer, take separate samples of both hot and cold water to your plumber, and he can test it for hardness on the spot.

Q: The chrome cups under the coils of my brand-new stove are becoming discolored, and there doesn't seem to be anything I can clean them with. Any suggestions?

R. B., Middlebury

A: We didn't know the answer, but Mary, of Clarendon, wrote us: "Many years ago we used something called Blueaway to clean up discoloration on exhaust pipes. As I cook with wood, I can't try it, but maybe R.B. would want to. We got it from motorcycle shops." It is also available from Associated Distributors, Inc., Palisades Park, NJ 07650 (800-421-5555).

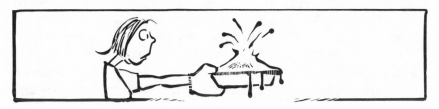

Q: When I bake pies they usually erupt over the top of the dish while they are baking. I know I should put a cookie tin beneath the pie plate, but I always forget. The floor of my oven is therefore a real mess. Have you any ideas that will make the clean-up easier?

Messy in Reading

A: Try sprinkling salt on any spillovers that occur while baking. (This is a good idea even if you remember the cookie sheet!) When the oven cools, you should be able to use a spatula to lift up the erupted filling.

POTS, PANS, ETC.

Q: I bought a Corning Ware teapot at a yard sale. The outside is perfect, but the inside must have been used to plant things. The surface is rough and discolored even after I've used scouring powder and put it repeatedly through the washing machine, in which I used Cascade. Two questions. One: is it safe to use the teapot for serving boiling water or for coffee? Two: is there any way to really get rid of the dark, rough spots?

M. T., Mt. Holly

A: First, a caution: never, never use scouring powder on Corning Ware surfaces. Instead use baking soda liberally sprinkled on a damp sponge or plastic "scratcher."

You don't tell us if the surface roughness is a result of pitting or if it is caused by deposits on the surface. If the latter, lime deposits may be causing the problem. They could also be the reason for the discoloration. To remove them fill the pot with one part white vinegar and one part water and boil vigorously for 15-20 minutes, empty the pot and scrub vigorously, first with a plastic scratcher and then with a damp cloth or sponge dipped in baking soda or dishwasher detergent. You may have to repeat this process two or three times. Incidentally, be sure the pot is rinsed clear of vinegar before you use the baking soda, as they cancel each other out.

In answer to your second question, if you still can't get the pot clean and if you don't know what the residue is, it's probably a better idea to stay on the safe side and not use it for boiling water.

READER FEEDBACK: J.P. wrote: "For the stain: I use Clorox on my coffee pot. Once a month I fill my nine-cup percolator with hot water, add about 1/4 cup of Clorox, and let stand. The stains disappear without scrubbing."

Q: I have a Melmac cereal dish stuck inside an oven-proof quart mixing bowl. Have you any suggestions as to how I can release the dish?

S. M. Wheeler, Bellows Falls

A: Our suggestion is based on the principles of thermal contraction and expansion. Put the mixing bowl in hot water to expand it. Put ice cubes in the Melmac bowl for contraction. When they have set a spell, give the two a good tug and they should come apart.

Q: Do you have any suggestions for bringing luster back to my "couth polymer" lowball glasses? I enjoy using them but am distressed to find that a dull appearance remains, whether the glasses are washed by hand or machine. How can I shine them up?

R. R. N., Springfield

A: The dull appearance may be caused by an oily film coating which plastic seems to attract and hold on to. It may also be caused by hard-water residue. In either case, dilute a cup of white vinegar with a quart of water and let the glasses soak a few minutes. Then wash with hot, soapy water and dry at once. If they still look dull, it's probably due to ordinary wear and tear. Polymer, as you know, is softer than glass and scratches more easily. Even nylon scrubber pads will leave minute scratches on a polymer surface.

Q: Is there anything that really works to clean the cooked-on oil on a corn popper? I used to use Ajax floor cleaner, which worked (with a little elbow grease), but they changed the formula, and it doesn't work any more.

R. L. Crandall, Windsor

A: We have a couple of suggestions. The first is to mix a generous tablespoon of Electrosol, Cascade or some other dishwasher detergent with hot water, put it in the popper and let soak overnight. This may work. The second is to apply Gunk to the cooked-on oil. Gunk is available in auto-supply stores and is used by mechanics to clean hardened grease and oil from engine parts. Gunk definitely will work, but be sure you wash the corn popper very, very thoroughly afterwards.

Q: I have several sizes of new iron skillets. What is the proper way to season and mantain them? Everyone I've asked has a different method. Is there a right way that is safe? Finally, is iron transferred to the food cooked in skillets like these, and if it is, is it harmful?

David Ferland, Middlesex

A: To season your iron skillets, coat the insides with unsalted fat or cooking oil and heat them in a 250-degree oven for several hours. After you've used them, don't soak, scour or put them in the dishwasher, but rinse and either wipe them dry, put them on the stove over low heat or, if you have a pilot light, put them in the oven. The mild heat will dry them thoroughly. To prevent rust make sure they are completely dry before you put them away: we don't stack ours, but hang them from hooks on the wall so that air can circulate around them. If you aren't going to be using a skillet for a while, wipe the inside with an oily paper towel. Yes, sometimes iron from a skillet is transferred to food, but it is not harmful.

Q: I have a Teflon pan I use in my oven that has gotten really grungy. I don't want to scrub it, but just ordinary washing doesn't get the baked-on oil off. Can you help?

Gretchen, Woodstock

A: We have three recipes. Warning: they should *never* be used in combination. With each one, put the mixture in the stained utensil and simmer for 15 minutes, either in the oven at high temperature or on top of the stove. Then wash thoroughly and season with a little bit of vegetable oil before using.

Recipe 1: ¼ cup coffee-pot cleaner in 1 quart water.
Recipe 2: 3 tablespoons dishwashing detergent in 1 cup water.
Recipe 3: 3 tablespoons oxygen bleach (powder form), 1 teaspoon light-duty liquid detergent, 1 cup water.

If there is some residue remaining, scrub with a soft pad.

Q: I am now on my third Wearever Silverstone Nonstick frying pan, and with each one I have found that after two or three months of use, the coating on the inside surface begins to peel off. When this happens I have thrown the pans away, as I am unsure if they are safe. Would eating the peeling be harmful? I always use a plastic spatula and clean the pans as directed. I would appreciate any information you have regarding this product.

Mrs. Richard Goodrum, Springfield

A: We are absolutely baffled by your report that the Silverstone peels off. Silverstone, unlike Teflon which is a coating, is a nonstick substance with which the metal of the pan is impregnated. It will scratch off under adverse circumstances, but will not peel. Anyway, while ingesting the peelings (or whatever) is not harmful, we imagine it is unpleasant knowing you are eating not only what is in your frying pan but what is on it as well. Our expert tells us that Wearever Silverstone, or any coated frying pan, will wear out eventually, but in two or three years rather than months. He reminded us that a coated frying pan, be it Teflon, or something else, is not an all-purpose pan and should only be used for simmering, light frying or sauteeing. The heat under the pan should never be higher than medium. This rather important piece of information is not, unfortunately, included in the directions for use that come with coated frying pans—at least not the ones we have purchased.

THE BATHROOM

Q: My vinyl shower curtain is disgusting. It's thick with soap and mildew. It was expensive, so I am reluctant to throw it out. Is there any way to clean it?

Anonymous, Randolph

A: Welcome to the ranks of owners of grungy shower curtains. We too have had the problem you describe, and we offer you a solution that worked for us. Put your curtain in the washing machine with two towels. Add ¹/₂ cup detergent and ¹/₂ cup baking soda. Add 1 cup vinegar to the last rinse. Don't spin, but remove immediately and hang.

Q: How do you clean the underside of a bathtub mat? I have used everything I can think of to clean around the suction cups. Good mats are expensive, and I'd like to find a way to keep the underside clean.

Mrs. Philip George, Barre

A: There is a product, available at TrueValue Hardware stores called Tru-Test Professional Cleaner. Although our source said that he uses the product to clean lawnmowers, it can be used on any surface that is not harmed by water. It sells for about $2 a quart.

READER FEEDBACK: Carole Wageman sent us a different solution for cleaning the underside of bathmats. "I submerge mine in cold water in the bathtub, gunky side up, and pour household bleach on it. A few swishes and a 10- to 15-minute soak have always cleaned it. I soak our bathtub scrub brush at the same time. In addition, bleach (diluted with a little water) in a spray bottle works similarly on mildewed bath tiles and caulking. Spray on, leave 10 or 15 minutes, and rinse. I also use this on mildew spots above the shower."

BATHTUBS AND SHOWERS

Q: I have porcelain fixtures in my bathroom. We have to leave the water running a little in the tub in the winter so the pipes won't freeze. Our water has a lot of lime in it. The lime coats the tub where the water spatters and collects in a pool. I can't find anything that will remove this deposit. Can you help me? I boil my kettle with a vinegar solution and that takes off the deposit.

B. Nichols, Randolph

A: We had the same problem with lime deposits until our plumber suggested a product called Lime-A-Way, which is available in hardware stores and some supermarkets. It has solved our lime build-up blues, and the label says it's a "nonabrasive liquid cleaner that quickly and easily dissolves lime, scale, rust and other hard-water deposits." Be sure and wear rubber gloves and test the cleaner on a tiny place first, for it may etch. We've never had a problem with this, however.

Q: I would like to know if anyone knows how to get a yellow stain off a bathtub?

Annie Shephard, Waterbury

A: There are two things you can try. The first is to rub the stain with a solution of salt and turpentine. Rinse well. Second, if the tub is extremely stained, use a mixture of peroxide (available from your druggist) and cream of tartar, made into a paste. Again, rinse thoroughly. If even that doesn't work, apply more paste and sprinkle on some household ammonia. Let sit a couple of hours, then rinse. Good luck!

Q: Please, what is the best way to remove bathtub decals?

Mary Dorman, Northfield

A: We use nail-polish remover. Apply around the edge of the decals and yank them up. Use more to remove the remaining glue.

Q: Help! We have an old Standard bathtub which at one time my husband wanted to replace. With loud protestations I managed to overrule him, and that nice, deep, soothing bathtub remains. Recently and suddenly, however, the bottom of the tub has become impossible to clean. On the bottom are what appear to be grayish stains. It is probably showing wear from years of abrasive cleaners. If I scrub and then soak for an hour or so in Clorox and hot water, the stains do disappear. Two or three days later, though, they are back. I don't want to resurface the entire tub. Is there a cleaner available that will do the trick?

Linda Matson, Rutland

A: We're afraid you'll have to refinish the bottom of your tub, but according to our friends at Vermont Salvage in Montpelier, it's no big deal. If you'll write A-Ball Plumbing Supply, 1703 W. Burnside St., Portland, OR 97209, they'll send you the materials you'll need as well as complete instructions.

Q: Do you know of anyone who refinishes tubs and lavatories? This process makes them look like new, and the finish is like an enamel.

Eleanor Paul, Rochester

A: If you don't want to do it yourself, you'll have to import someone from New York State. Mike Opalka of Empire Ceramic Tub Refinishing, Coeymans, NY 12045 (518-475-2868), comes to Vermont when he gets enough requests to make it worth the trip. (When we called him he had just returned from Fort Leonard Wood in Missouri, where he had refinished about a zillion tubs.) Dorothy Woods, of Pittsford, sent in the name of another refinisher who she says does beautiful work: Richard Mack, Box 96, Amsterdam, NY 12010 (518-842-2534).

Q: Please! What will cut the soap film and clean a shower stall and glass shower doors? The product must not be toxic or harmful to the lungs.

Phyl Merritt, Montpelier

A: Dissolve ½ cup of Arm & Hammer Washing Soda in 2 quarts boiling water. Cool to comfortable temperature. Wring out a soft cloth or sponge in this mixture, sprinkle a little more washing soda on the cloth and rub the glass vigorously. Rinse with clear water; dry with an old towel. This works equally well on bathtub tile. Use rubber gloves, as the mixture is somewhat harsh.

TOILETS

Q: How does one stop a bathroom toilet bowl from sweating? Ours even wets the floor.

Rutland Resident

A: Are you sure the bowl itself is sweating? Is it possible that the seal between the bowl and the floor has become worn, and the water is leaking from the base of the toilet? The reason we ask is that it is the tank portion of the toilet rather than the bowl which is prone to sweating. The reason for sweat forming (and this is usually a summer rather than a winter problem) is that the humid outside air is appreciably warmer than the water inside the tank. As warm air hits the cold porcelain, condensation occurs. This can be solved either by installing an insulating liner in the tank, which comes in kit form and can be purchased from your plumber for around $10, or by having your plumber install a tempering valve which will allow a small amount of hot water into the tank every time you flush and so overcome the temperature difference that promotes condensation.

Q: Can you tell me how to get black scratches out of the inside of a toilet bowl caused by the metal ring on a brush? I've tried dish detergent, SOS pads, Comet, Clorox. Nothing works.

A. R., Rutland

A: Shortly after we received this letter,. B.W. Sheflin, of Killington, sent us this feedback. We think his suggestion may solve your problem: "A couple of weeks ago someone asked how to get a blue line, caused by using Ty-D Bol, off their toilet bowl. We had this problem and tried everything without success. After a couple of months, it occurred to me to try a product we have around to take iron deposits out of the water softener. It removed enough of the blue line so it is barely visible. The product is Super Iron Out. The label says it is 'an all-purpose rust and stain remover.' Large plumbing-supply houses should have it in stock, and also people who sell and service water softeners.

"We lowered the level of the bowl by dumping in a pail of water and then wet the bowl and with a spoon applied the Super Iron Out to the line. After a few minutes we used an old washcloth to rub the powder around. A word of caution: people should not use scouring powder in toilet bowls, as it roughens the enamel surface and then you have a lifetime cleaning problem."

FIBERGLASS

Q: What does one use to clean the new fiberglass bathtub/shower units? I've tried all the "old" products like Soft Scrub, Comet, etc., not to mention vinegar and bleach. Nothing seems to get my unit absolutely white again.

J. M., Hardwick

A: We didn't own a fiberglass shower unit at the time we received this letter and didn't know the answer. Fortunately many readers came up with suggestions. Lucille Aja, of Barre, wrote, "I have discovered a great product for cleaning fiberglass. It is manufactured by the Dow Chemical Company and is called Tough Act. It comes in a spray bottle; just spray it on and then wipe off with a soft plastic scrubber. One word of advice: if you find it and like it, I would recommend buying a full year's supply, as any product I recommend is usually removed from the shelves with a speed in direct proportion to the enthusiasm with which I recommend it! In the last six months alone I have seen the demise of three candy bars, the best bra slip ever made and numerous other articles." (As of this writing—much, we are sure, to Ms. Aja's surprise and relief—Tough Act is still widely available.)

"Tried Everything in Washington" wrote: "Make a paste of baking soda and scrub with a Teflon scouring pad. Also baking soda is great for your septic system, so you kill two birds with one stone."

"A Rutland Reader" is very enthusiastic about a product called FC-301, Mineral and Millstone Removal and Alternate Daily Cleaner sold in one-gallon jugs for about $9. "Just spray it on and wait and watch the dirt and scum run off after about 20 minutes. You may need two or three applications the first time, but it works. The odor will asphyxiate you, so ventilate well. I purchase the jug locally from a fellow who sells to dairy farmers. This solution, which is really a bulk milk tank cleaner and is nontoxic, can be bought from other farm suppliers too."

CHAPTER 2

HOUSEHOLD UPKEEP

Every once in a while we get a hint that answers a question we have never been able to answer to anyone's (including our own) satisfaction. Over the years we've had more questions about lime residue than we can count—not surprising, as the majority of our readers live in Vermont where the water is so hard you can bounce off it. We've come up with a million suggestions, from marbles to Lime-A-Way. Who would ever have thought that the ultimate answer would be Polident tablets?

ALUMINUM

Q: My husband built a slide for our son. He used aluminum flashing for the sliding surface. Our son gets very dirty sliding on it—gray-black stains on clothes and body. Is there anything that can be done to the aluminum so that he doesn't get dirty?

Bonnie, Brandon

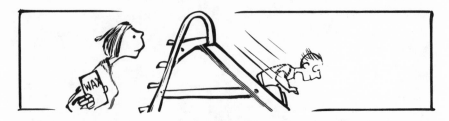

A: Every time your son goes down the slide, he's polishing off a thin layer of oxidation. We suggest that you first clean the surface of the slide with paint thinner, then polish with a cloth until there is no more gray-black residue. Cover with two coats of a hard carnuba wax, such as Turtle Wax for cars. Polish after both the first and second applications. If the wax doesn't work you may want to paint the slide with Rustoleum enamel spray paint, but the wax will be more fun for your son. It's slipperier!

Q: What can I use on aluminum siding to remove streaks, stains and other marks? What is best?

Ira K. Blackbird, Fair Haven

A: The product you use depends on whether you have repainted the aluminum siding since it was put it on the house. If you have, we recommend you use a mild detergent (Ivory Liquid or other dishwashing detergent), as anything stronger could harm the paint. Make a suds and scrub the siding with a soft brush. If the siding hasn't been repainted, aluminum siding cleaner is available at most hardware stores. It contains potassium hydroxide and should be used with extreme care.

WOOD FLOORS

Q: The floors in my house are of a soft wood and have been painted. I have found that most products used to clean them cause a film. I have used Spic and Span, Murphy's, Pine Sol and liquid Lysol. All of these products leave a dull film on the floor, which makes the floor look worse. I really don't want to use plain hot water, as I feel it won't do a good enough cleaning job. Any suggestions?

J. K. Oakman, Poultney

A: The solution is quite simple. After washing, rinse your floors thoroughly with clean, hot water and your problem should be solved.

CEMENT FLOORS AND STEPS

Q: My basement floor is painted cement, which gives me a problem every spring when moisture causes a white bloom which ruins the painted surface. I have tried sealers, to no avail. Can you tell me what to do or where I can get help?

Discouraged, Montpelier

A: Your problem is due to hydrostatic pressure, which is particularly strong in the spring when the ground is saturated with water. If your foundation was poured without adequate exterior drainage, even a millimeter's gap between wall and slab will allow moisture to creep in, thus ruining your paint job. All the sealer in the world won't help as water is not coming up through the concrete (concrete is not porous) but is forcing its way between the wall and the slab and moving over the slab surface in a thin film. There is nothing you can do on your own about this problem: we suggest you look for advice in the Yellow Pages under Concrete Contractors. Be sure, as always, to get more than one opinion!

Q: Our car leaked motor oil over the entire garage floor. It has spread into our laundry room (which also has a cement floor) and out onto the dirt, snow-and-ice-covered driveway. Any suggestions as to what to do to keep from tracking it in and also clean the oil up?

Disgruntled, Rutland

A: We suggest you buy a large bag of Florco-X Absorbent, a cat litter-like material that is oil-absorbent. You can buy it at most automotive and farm-supply stores. Spread it around and leave for a few days. It may take two or three applications, but the material will eventually pull the oil off the cement. If for some reason all the oil isn't removed, experiment with some paint thinner on the stubborn places. Using Florco-X outside is worthless, as it absorbs water: a good layer of sand is probably your best bet till spring thaw, when the oil should wash away of its own accord.

Q: Could you please tell me how to remove moss that is growing on my cement steps, roof and cedar deck furniture?

Howard Loso, Rutland

A: We asked the advice of an old friend of ours, who has lived most of her life in the damp and humid environment of Hawaii. "We just scrub things down with bleach," she said. "The stronger the solution, the better." We hated to think of you crawling around on your roof with a bucket and a brush and so called the Extension Service. Our Agent laughed and said that in Vermont there didn't seem to be a big enough moss problem to warrant any literature on it. He suggested a good dose of sun would probably do the trick.

CAST IRON

Q: Our black cast-iron wood-stove kettle is filled with lime scale. Is there a solution? I have tried Lime-A-Way and it doesn't work.

Eugenia, Castleton

A: Fill your kettle with white vinegar and let it sit for at least 24 hours. You may have to scrub it a little bit at the end, but it should come clean. To prevent scale buildup, buy some marbles at your toy counter and put a handful in the bottom of the kettle. Boiling water will cause the marbles to jump around and knock against the sides and bottom of the kettle, which will prevent lime residue from accumulating. (This also will work to keep your tea kettle or glass coffee pot lime free.)

Q: I am the proud but discouraged owner of a cast-iron sink. I was told it should be kept oiled, as a cast-iron frying pan is. Unfortunately the oil tends to turn nasty and black—sometimes after just 24 hours—and to disappear in spots which then immediately rust. I've scrubbed the sink clean of all oil and rust and sprayed with a clear acrylic, but to no avail. The acrylic left a white residue and was gone in a day! Do you know of any way to keep this wonderful old sink looking clean for at least a week?

Barbara Wolf, Bethel

A: 1. Take steel wool and rub the sink down until entirely clean and free of rust.

2. Dry with a towel and then with a hair dryer.
3. Rub suet or uncured pork fat into sink surface (and rub and rub!) so that the microgrooves in the cast iron are permeated.
4. Repeat every day over the next week. If you have to use the sink, don't let water sit in it and dry after each use. If you don't care about authenticity, you can coat the sink with a marine-grade urethane, but it will eventually begin to chip, and you'll have to start all over again.

READER FEEDBACK: A faithful reader wrote: "My mother used to put a few drops of kerosene on wadded-up newspaper and rub the sink. It kept it from rusting and gave a nice shine."

CHIMNEYS

Q: We had an air-tight stove in our house, and it and the chimney (which was from the fireplace) became so filled with creosote that we have had to take out the stove. We would like to be able to use the fireplace, but the chimney is full of this sticky mess—gobs or hard "whatever" that we cannot move. Brushes and chains won't touch it. This is a one-story house, and so the chimney isn't long. We have asked several people—firemen, cleaners, etc.—and get various suggestions. "Burn it out." "No, you'll burn down your house"—things like that. No good suggestions. Surely with all the woodstoves being used, we can't be the only people with this problem. Two years ago we had a chimney fire.

Doris Lowre, North Bennington

A: The burning questions are: when you had your chimney fire, did the flue tile become cracked and damaged? Did you have the chimney relined? (It might have been covered by your homeowner's policy if 1.) the tile was damaged, and 2.) you filed a claim.) If your flue tile is intact, look in the Yellow Pages and call a chimney-sweeping service: ask them if they can give you the name of someone in the state who has the training to "flake" a chimney. As of this writing the only person we know in Vermont who can "flake" has given up cleaning chimneys for the more lucrative business of selling real estate. "Flaking" is, as far as we know, the only way you are going to get your chimney clean. It is a special technique which comes from Germany and involves burning off the creosote from the top of the chimney flue down. Our second suggestion is that you look again in the Yellow Pages, for the chimney cleaning/repair company nearest you that uses Thermocrete flue liner. We were told by a couple of sources that a Thermocrete lining can be poured right over the existing creosote. The process involves inflating an air bag in your chimney and then pouring Thermocrete, under pressure, around its sides.

BRASS

Q: Last year at a craft fair I bought a kind of chunky brass neck chain. I wore it until it started tarnishing. I tried polishing it with Brasso but couldn't get it clean between the links. It looks terrible. Any suggestions?

S. B., Reading

A: The craftsperson from whom you bought the jewelry apparently didn't believe in lacquering his or her product. Lacquering is both a good and a bad thing: good because it keeps the brass from tarnishing and bad because once the lacquer wears off, no amount of polishing will make the necklace look like new. It has to be relacquered. There is a solution to your problem, although it sounds a trifle bizarre. Take a packet of orange Kool-Aid and dilute according to instructions. Drop your necklace in and leave it to soak until the tarnish has disappeared. Wash with a mild detergent and rinse in very hot water. Dry at once with a soft cloth.

Q: A few years ago I had some brass candlesticks and lamp bases lacquered so they would not have to be polished so often. Now they look dull and dirty. Can you recommend something that will safely remove the lacquer without damaging the brass?

J. Estes, Poultney

A: There are two methods you can use. One is to soak the pieces in hot soapy water for about 15 minutes. Rinse with hot water and rub with a soft cloth until the lacquer peels away. The second method is to rub the piece with a soft cloth moistened with denatured alcohol.

Q: Back when I was very young (am now 71) they used to give out coupons with Octagon soap. My aunt got a brass bed with hers. She passed away a few years ago, and I have the bed. What I would like to know is if there is any way to clean it besides Brasso? I'm not too happy with the results with Brasso and it doesn't last very long. Someone told me to use, I think, Valspar varnish after the bed was cleaned, but I'm afraid to use it.

Blanche Graves, Springfield

A: It is perfectly safe to use an acrylic finish such as Valspar, a lacquer or a tung oil product to keep your bed from tarnishing. These products can either be brushed, sprayed, or in the case of tung oil, rubbed on.

Before you apply any finish, make sure your brass bed is clean. If you don't want to use Brasso, you can make a cleaning paste of equal parts salt, vinegar and flour. Then cook up the following to give your brass a good shine: heat 2 cups of water to a boil and add 1/2 cup soap flakes. Stir to dissolve. While continuing to stir, add 3 tablespoons Paris white (also called whiting and available at paint and hardware stores) and 2 tablespoons white vinegar. Beat with hand or electric mixer; store any left over in a clean glass jar and shake well before using. These two recipes can also be used to clean copper.

COPPER, PEWTER AND SILVER

Q: Some years ago I bought some bronze tableware in Thailand, and as of now I have found nothing that will polish it. I have tried copper and silver polish of various brands as well as Noxon, Zud and some other all-purpose polishes with no success. Can you suggest something?

Henry Chapman, Dorset

A: We are going to go on the assumption that the bronze has not been lacquered. The bronze/copper alloy your tableware is made of can be harmed by: air pollutants, the common home polish of lemon and salt and some commercial products, particularly those containing ammonia. Our expert in these matters suggests you do the following: first, clean the bronze with alcohol and a cotton swab. This will remove finger oils, perspiration, etc. Then concoct a homemade polish of two parts denatured alcohol, two parts distilled water and enough precipitated chalk (available at jewelry and dental-supply stores) to make a thick paste. You can, if you wish, substitute rottenstone (available at paint stores) or jeweler's rouge for the chalk.

Q: I have some old pewter porringers, and I haven't had any luck cleaning them with commercial polishes. Do you know of a home-made polish I can use?

E. W., Corinth

A: If you are concerned with the resale value of your pewter, most collectors recommend that you not polish it but instead give it an occasional wash with soapy, warm water. If it has gotten very dirty, pewter with a dull finish can be cleaned by rubbing with a fine steel wool pad (Number 0000) and olive oil, with a moist paste of wood ash and water, or with toothpaste and a damp cloth. An old-fashioned way to clean pewter is to rub moist cabbage leaves over the surface, then buff with a soft cloth.

To clean pewter with a shiny finish, make a paste from isopropyl alcohol (70 percent) and whiting (available at most hardware and paint stores). Coat the entire surface with the paste and allow to dry. Then polish with a soft cloth.

Q: What is the best way to remove pitting on sterling silver, besides prolonged rubbing with silver polish?

Winifred T. Bouvet, Montpelier

A: This is a problem we recently solved with a combination of elbow grease and the purchase of a Sonic Silver Cleaner made by Invento. It costs about $30 and is designed for silverware, although it will accommodate small things like salt shakers and pepper grinders. It helped loosen the dark pits on our silver, but prolonged rubbing was also necessary. We asked our jeweler about other options. He said a cloth buffing wheel and some jeweler's rouge would also do the trick, but using them is time-consuming.

FEATHERS AND DRIED FLOWERS

Q: I have a nice centerpiece of feathers: orange, yellow and brown. They are dusty and soiled. How can I clean them?

M. R. V., Barre

A: If your centerpiece can be dismantled, take the feathers and lay them flat on a sheet of white paper or a piece of cloth. Sprinkle them generously with table salt so their entire surface is covered, and let them sit for a while. Then take a soft brush, such as a baby's hairbrush, and brush them off. Turn over and repeat the process on the other side.

Table salt also works well for cleaning dried flowers that have become dusty and grungy. Put the flowers head down in a paper bag, pour in a generous amount of table salt and swish them around gently a few times. You'll be surprised how dirty the table salt gets, and how clean your flowers become!

HUMIDIFIERS

Q: I have a sonic humidifier, and my water is very hard. The humidifier cakes up with lime and doesn't work properly. There are cleaners on the market, but they are very expensive. Any hints you could give me to keep it clean?

K. A., Berlin

A: Mix equal parts of white vinegar and water and fill the chamber of your humidifier; turn on to the High setting. By the time the chamber is empty, your humidifier will be clean. We suggest you put it outdoors while performing this process, or your house will smell very strongly of vinegar. For regular humidifiers, put a copper scouring pad in the bottom of the tank. Add a dollop of household bleach to the water. This should eliminate both lime or mineral build-up and odor caused by bacteria.

LIME RESIDUE (WHITE FILM)

Q: I have a crystal pepper shaker and would like to know how I can get the film out of the inside when I want to clean it. I have tried soaking it in warm water, in baking soda, putting it through the dishwasher, etc. Please give me some help with this problem.

A: Take a little dishwasher detergent such as Calgonite, put it in your shaker along with some hot water and let it sit overnight. If this doesn't work, you can try a product called Lime-A-Way, available at supermarkets and hardware stores.

READER FEEDBACK: Mary MacMahon, of Brandon, sent us the following Superhint: "In the past, I have seen many requests in your column for info regarding cleaning decanters, vases, etc. In many years I used everything I ever heard of (including Lime-A-Way) with no success. Then I heard of the following, and I will say, it is always wonderful for this problem: Polident Denture Cleanser! Fill the decanter or vase or whatever with water and drop one tablet in. Let stand for ½ to 1 hour; then wash and rinse as usual. I'm sure your many readers who have had this problem will be delighted with Polident!"

MARBLE

Q: How do you clean an old marble or alabaster lamp?

C. B., Londonderry

A: If it's very dirty, scour with a paste of baking soda and water. Let stand a few minutes and rinse. If it's a question of just ordinary grime, sprinkle salt on a lemon half and wipe over the surface. Rinse off with soap and water. If you wish to put a shine on the lamp, use a paste carnuba wax. Oil polishes or soft waxes will cause discoloration.

STICK-UM

Q: Any ideas how to clean window frames of the residue that is left over from the plastic interior-window kits that use double-edge clear tape to install? It's still sticky after you remove the old tape, which prevents the next year's tape from adhering well.

A. S., Montpelier

A: We found that Goop Hand Cleaner does a wonderful job: put some on a cloth and wipe away. If the stick-um proves particularly stubborn, just spread some Goop on and let it sit for a couple of minutes. Incidentally, we have been using Goop all winter to rid our hands of the smell of kerosene which lingers long after we have filled our lamps and lit our fires. The stuff is wonderful and has a thousand uses. Don't know how we lived without it!

Q: I clean second homes. Many of them are new construction. The problem is getting stickers off new appliances: washers, dryers, stoves, refrigerators and especially fiberglass showers. You might be able to get the paper layer off but all the sticky residue is left. Because of the new types of surfaces you can't use scouring powders or even Teflon pads, as they dull the surface.

Mary C. Law, Wilmington

A: For metal, glass or wood surfaces, you have a number of options. TrueValue hardware stores carry a product called Fast 'N Easy Sticker Remover. Available at ServiStar and other hardware stores is Weldwood Cleaner and Thinner. Also a stick-um remover, it is particularly recommended for the removal of labels from plastic surfaces. In many cases, Crisco or vegetable oil will also do the trick. One reader recommended peanut butter. Another suggested a product called Thin-X (mineral spirits), which he uses with a small brush to clean up glue residue. We have used WD-40, which is a super-lubricant (available at automotive stores) with great success.

For stick-um on fiberglass, saturate a clean white rag with nail-polish remover. You don't need a lot: rub until label adhesive disappears. Don't allow any remover to go down the drain or collect on the grate of the drain; if you use enough so this happens, you are using too much. Remember that nail-polish remover is highly flammable and no one should even think of smoking in the room where it's used.

A note about fiberglass: if you apply a good automotive wax on the shower/tub surface and buff it with a towel to a high shine, the surface will be much easier to keep clean!

Superhint: Eleanor Marsh, of Poultney, sent us this one. "The other day I picked up a bagful of lovely, pitchy white pine cones for Christmas crafts, and my hands were so covered with pitch that I could hardly get back into the house. I reached for the faithful nail-polish remover, but there was so much pitch it just made mud. In desperation I grabbed the bottle nearest the nail polish remover, which just happened to be salad oil, poured it over my hands over the sink, rubbed it all over and wiped it off with paper towels. My hands were so lovely, soft and clean I didn't even wash them! Have other pine-cone crafters discovered this lovely secret? I now use salad oil on sticky labels on jars I want to save."

SMOKE AND FIRE

Q: Our home recently burned, and everything was burned or ruined. The unburned items are covered with a thick black residue. What can I use to get my things clean?

S. West, Pawlet

A: The Rutland Fire Clay Company has introduced a product called Hearth Glass Conditioning Cleaner formulated to dissolve creosote and stove polish. The man we talked with at the firm assured us that this product was just right for cleaning smoke residue. You can write or call the company for the dealer nearest you: Perkins Rd., Rutland, VT 05701 (802-775-7654).

VARNISH

Q: I have a nice varnished dining room table, and I put a flannel-backed cloth on to protect it, as we spend a lot of time at it writing letters and watching TV. The flannel came off on the table, and I can't get it off.

Mrs. Frank Pryor, Barre

A: We don't hold out a lot of hope that this will work, as the flannel is probably pretty well embedded in the varnish, which softens under the slightest exposure to heat. Try this method on a small area before doing the entire table. Warm up a quantity of either boiled linseed oil or light mineral oil and saturate the surface. Let the oil sit for a while and then, using a Number-0000 steel-wool pad, rub carefully and slowly with the grain of the wood. Wipe with a dry cloth to polish.

WINDOWS

Q: Can you tell me the best solution for washing windows? A solution of bleach? Ammonia? Vinegar? Are there different kinds of glass that take different treatments?

M. B., Hardwick

A: An ammonia solution for washing windows in the house is the best. Use ¼ cup ammonia to 2 cups hot water. Add a drop or two of dish detergent. Do not use this solution on tinted glass, as it will pull the tint out. A few tips: never wash windows when the sun is shining on them, as they'll dry too fast and streak. Use a cheap chamois, old nylons or newspaper to wipe with. We like newspaper the best, as there seems to be something in the ink that really shines the glass. When you polish your windows use an up-and-down stroke on one side and side to side strokes on the other. This way you can tell which side needs extra polishing.

For the outside surfaces of large-paned windows, Virginia Rivers, of Forest Dale, sent us the following tip. "Take a pail of hot water and add enough cider vinegar so it smells strong. Take a sponge mop and scrub windows down with this solution. Then take a hose and hose down the windows. No need to wipe, as the windows dry streak-free. Also this will not harm flowers, plants or shrubs."

WOOD

Q: What can be done to restore finish to plywood paneling? With years of age it is beginning to wear around knobs, and in some places small hairline cracks appear.

Mrs. B. L. J., Manchester

A: We think your best solution is to use a wood filler such as Bix Stain Putty, which you can mix with a stain to get the right color. You can finish off the restoration with a polyurethane sealer.

READER FEEDBACK: John Olson, of Rutland, wrote, "There is a product on the market called The Solution. The difference between that and polyurethane is that The Solution feeds and restores moisture to the wood. It's available at most hardware and paint stores."

Q: We have an old barn beam for our mantel over the fireplace. Candles dripped on it, and after removing the wax I find I cannot remove the oils left from the wax. Any suggestions?

N. C., Pittsford

A: What you need is a strong grease solvent: TSP (trisodium phosphate) should do the trick. Follow the directions carefully and use rubber gloves. You may end up with some residue, so (carefully again) rub with lighter fluid. Then oil the beam with any kind of finishing oil that will penetrate the wood: linseed, vegetable or mineral oils are all fine. The oil not only gives a uniform finish to the beam but is good for the wood as well.

Q: I have two really nice wooden salad bowls. They have become sticky. How can I clean them properly? How can I prevent the stickiness from recurring?

A. T. Comstock, Tunbridge

A: We spoke with the experts at the Weston Bowl Mill in Weston. They said there is little hope for your problem, as salad oil over time has saturated the wood. They suggest you scrub the bowls with very hot water and detergent—and really scrub! Do not soak, as this will cause the bowls to crack. When and if you have removed the stickiness, give the bowls a light wipe or two with mineral oil and let stand a couple of days so that the oil has a chance to penetrate. In the future, after using, give your bowls a quick wash with soapy water, rinse and dry well.

RADIATORS

Q: I live in an apartment building with steam heat. I've never lived with radiators, and now that cold weather is here I am blasted out of bed every morning when the pipes start pounding. Why does it happen? Is there anything that can be done to stop it? The landlord says there isn't.

Pipe Dreams, Barre

A: The banging in hot water and steam pipes is called "water hammer" or "hydraulic shock." Water is incompressible and acts like a hammer when a valve is closed. Flowing water hits against the closed valve and bangs the pipe. There is nothing to be done about these early morning sounds when the steam or hot water suddenly starts flowing into cold pipes. If the banging persists throughout the day, however, it could be caused by a partially closed valve, high pressure, or the radiator's being tipped the wrong way.

READER FEEDBACK: David Merritt, of Springfield, wrote that he had his plumber lower the steam pipe over the furnace to get better drainage from the radiators. He also put a ¹/₂-inch block under the radiator legs opposite the steam valve to get quicker drainage of the condensed steam.

SEPTIC SYSTEMS

Q: Do you know anything about the practice of occasionally adding baker's yeast to a septic system to promote the breakdown of waste? Does it really have an effect, and if so, what's the proper method of doing it?

Mary McCallum, Cavendish

A: Our plumber tells us that in the olden days, when septic tanks were smaller and made of metal rather than concrete, people did in fact add yeast. He noted that he didn't know how effective it actually was in those days, but with the larger, more efficient tanks that began to be used 20 years ago, it is definitely unnecessary. He added that if your septic tank is over 20 years old (i.e., of the metal variety) you should consider replacing it before it caves in: it is probably well on its way to self-destructing from advanced rust. If, despite all the above, you still want to add yeast to your septic system, flush 1 cake or 1 tablespoon of yeast down the toilet every six months.

SLATE ROOFS

Q: I have an old house with a slate roof which has to be replaced. I have heard there are people around that will take the slate off in return for keeping the slate. Do you know anything about this?

B. J. K., Randolph

A: There are not only people around who will take off the slate for the slate: there are people who will take off the slate and pay you for it! There are a few catches, however. The slate has to be worth it—i.e., good slate in good condition. Black slate from Pennsylvania is, for instance, of such poor quality that no one would want it, whereas the unfading colored slate from the Poultney-West Rutland area is in great demand. (This is probably what you have on your roof, given your address.) You want to get an extremely reputable person to do the work. There are a lot of shady characters around who will promise you everything, take the slate, leave a mess and deliver nothing in return. By the way, Mike Heffernan, at Red Dragon Slating in Calais, said he hopes you got "the real story" from whoever told you you need a new roof. Very often, repairing a slate roof will be only slightly more expensive than putting on a new tin or shingle roof, with the added advantage that the slate will last another 100 years.

CHAPTER 3

STAIN AND ODOR REMEDIES

Mildew? In Vermont? Thinking that mildew only occurs in Bermuda and poorly ventilated and tree-surrounded houses (such as ours) we have discovered that mildew is an on-going problem for everyone. Nan, who has a floored cellar and lives in a great rambling "summer cottage," and Anne, who has a dirt cellar and lives in an ancient farmhouse, suffer equally with those who live in ranch houses and apartments, suburbs and cities. Our conclusion is that mildew must not respect persons, climes or habitats. Except maybe in the Sahara—and we haven't gotten a letter from there to prove to the contrary. Yet.

DYE, MAGIC MARKER AND CRAYON

Q: My son wore a new pair of red pants out to play on a damp morning and now the vinyl trim on his sneakers is bright pink and resists all my efforts to remove it. Can you help me?

Deborah Reed, Hubbardton

36

A: Red is one of the hardest dyes to remove, as anyone who has mixed a red sock in with a white wash can attest. Try a strong solution of liquid bleach liberally applied and then scrubbed with an old toothbrush. You might also try Turtle Wax Vinyl Top Cleaner (for vinyl car tops). We use it to clean all kinds of vinyl (including lawn furniture) in and around the house, but you may not want to buy a whole can for one pair of sneakers.

Our final suggestion is that you scrub the sneakers with Colgate toothpaste. Years ago, when one of our children decided to decorate some antique paneling with indelible red marker, we were advised by our grandmother that giving him away to the gypsies wouldn't solve anything in the long run and that the seemingly permanent scrawls could be removed with a generous application of Colgate toothpaste, rubbed in with a soft cloth. It worked! (And will also work to remove crayon scribbles.)

FIREPLACE ODOR

Q: We have a camp on Lake Champlain that is 30 to 35 years old. It has a large fieldstone fireplace that is really great. However when the fireplace is not in use we frequently get a very unpleasant odor from it. Do you have any hints on how to get rid of this odor?

V. M., Orwell

A: The "very unpleasant odor" is caused by flammable creosote deposits mixing with humidity from the summer air and, in this case, from Lake Champlain. A thorough chimney cleaning, which should be done every year anyway, will reduce the odor a lot. Rutland Fireplace Deodorant or Copperfield Chimney and Fireplace Deodorant, sold at most wood-stove shops, will absorb the remaining odors. We also recommend a deodorized clay-type cat litter for wood stoves. Clean out the ashes and spread an inch or an inch and a half of cat litter in the stove. If you would like the name of the certified chimney sweep nearest you, send an SSAE to Vermont Chimney Sweep Guild, P.O. Box 191, East Wallingford, VT 05742.

FOOD ODORS

Q: How do you get a foul, fishy odor from the freezer section of a refrigerator? We were away for a few days, and the fridge stopped and a haddock fillet thawed. We've tried soda and vinegar, vanilla and good old soap and water, and it is still tainted.

C. W. Tucker, Graniteville

A: Scrub the interior thoroughly, paying special attention to the gaskets on the door and front of the freezer. A strong solution of chlorine bleach and hot water should do it. Then fill a bowl with powdered charcoal (the kind used for plants and aquarium filters) or with powdered instant coffee and put in the freezer. For deodorizing a cooler, follow the above steps and then saturate a cloth with vanilla and wipe down the insides. Leave the cloth in the cooler overnight.

MILDEW

Q: We're summer Vermonters who leave some clothes here over the winter. Can mildew be removed from pants and a jacket? How? We want to leave more clothes here over the winter. How can we avoid the problem?

Resident, Mt. Holly

A: Molds and mildews are simple plants belonging to the fungus family. They flourish wherever conditions are damp, poorly aired and/or poorly lighted. Make sure your clothes are thoroughly cleaned and aired before you store them and that drawers and closets have been thoroughly washed with Lysol and water to eliminate the chance that any mold spores may be lingering from the winter before. Dampness is the biggest problem. Silica gel or activated alumina will absorb moisture. Paraformaldehyde, which is sold in powder form in drugstores, may be sewn into sachet-type bags and placed in drawers and closets. Finally there is a product called De-Moist that consists of granular diatomaceous earth and calcium chloride. It comes already bagged and ready to use. It is frequently available in larger hardware stores.

For the jacket and pants that already have mildew on them, take them outside into the sun and brush thoroughly. If the fabric is nonwashable, take to the cleaners. If washable, moisten the mildewed areas with lemon juice and salt, put in the sun to dry, then rinse and dry again. Use with care on colored fabrics.

Q: How do you get a mildew smell out of a basement? The cement has wall-to-wall carpet on it and it got wet when the water tank leaked. We turned our heat up to dry it out, but we still get a mildew smell.

M. H. G., Barre

A: Heat alone will not kill the fungus spores that are growing in your carpet and causing the mildew smell. We are afraid there is nothing you can do but take the carpet up, put it outside in the sun and let it air. Mildew hates the sun and will obligingly die when exposed.

While the carpet is outside, get down on your hands and knees (sorry) and scrub the floor with hot water and Lysol or chlorine bleach. The important thing is that you get up any remaining mildew spores. Before you lay the carpet back down make sure it and the floor are absolutely dry.

Q: We have recently bought an older home and are bothered by an odor. It's a musty smell. The basement has a dirt floor. I've talked to many people who have the same problem and are anxious to find a solution. Someone suggested a wood stove in the basement to dry it up.

L. M., Sharon

A: The musty odors are caused by organisms breeding in the dampness of your cellar floor. The most effective solution is to lay down a vapor barrier and pour a concrete floor. The second is to spread chloride of lime throughout the basement (or, to be accurate, the cellar: in Vermont *basements* have concrete floors, and *cellars* have dirt floors). A cautionary note: if your house is an old one (late 18th- to mid-19th century) with a stone foundation, you should probably think twice before pouring a floor, especially if your cellar gets wet in the spring. In a couple of years you'll start running into all kinds of problems and may have to excavate around the foundation and put in drainage tile.

You might consider, as a third possibility, whitewashing your cellar walls, as lime is highly odor-absorbent. The recipe for whitewash is: 5 pounds quicklime, $1/2$ pound salt and $1/2$ pound sulfur. Add water slowly to the lime until it starts bubbling and heating due to the chemical reaction of lime and water. When the bubbling stops, but while the mixture is still hot, add a little more water and the rest of the ingredients. The final consistency should be that of wall primer paint.

A wood stove would not be effective, as heat alone will neither kill the organisms nor sufficiently dry the floor to discourage them. Remember, the dampness is coming up through, and not over, the floor.

Q: I have three musty leather suitcases. I have tried keeping bars of soap in them and different sachets. Nothing seems to work. The musty odor is always present.

M., Barre

A: The musty smell is due to mold or mildew, which can be present in such small (but malodorous) amounts that you can't see it. The best way to get rid of the smell is to air your suitcases in the sun for a day. Sponge the leather with equal amounts of rubbing alcohol and water, and wipe the fabric inside with lemon juice and water. When you bring the suitcases in at night, sprinkle deodorized clay-type cat litter in them and close them up. The final step is to fill a couple of old stockings with cedar chips to keep in the suitcases when you aren't using them.

Finally, to prevent a recurrence of the problem, store your suitcases in a place where there is good air circulation. Closets, which have very little ventilation, aren't good places to store them, nor are basements, which tend to be dark and damp. We keep ours in the attic and have never had any "musty" problems.

Q: I have a problem I've not seen in other household-hint articles. The smell of mildew is very strong in my washer. I have tried mildew spray, vinegar and deodorizers, and nothing has helped.

G. B., Chester

A: We went to see our lonely Maytag repairman who told us the following: Most washers have an inner and an outer basket, and sometimes a small piece of clothing, such as a sock, will find its way between them and start to mildew. The only solution (unless you have a mechanical mind and a full set of instructions) is to call a repairman, who will remove the inner basket and extract the garment.

He also suggested that, if your machine is a top loader, something may have gotten caught under the spindle that rotates the clothes. You can check that yourself by unscrewing the top of the spindle and lifting it out of the machine.

THERMOS STAINS AND ODORS

Q: My husband takes to work with him each day a two-quart stainless-steel Thermos bottle filled with coffee. He adds to this some regular milk. Our problem is that before the week is out the bottle gets very sour. Liquid detergent, etc., do not keep it sweet, and it is very, very difficult to rinse out. What can I do to clean it?

Greta, Plainfield

A: There are two fail-proof ways to get your husband's Thermos bottle squeaky clean. The first is, every evening after you wash the bottle out, put in a little Dip-It coffee percolator cleaner, fill with boiling water and watch all the brown gunk bubble up! The second is to drop a denture-cleaning tablet such as Polident into the bottle, fill with hot water and let sit overnight. No muss, no fuss.

PINE PITCH AND STICKY STUFF

Q: Pitch dripped from our Christmas tree onto our nylon carpeting, leaving a dark, hard stain. Could you recommend anything which might remove it?

Vera Strong, Northfield

A: Rub denatured alcohol into the offending spots. Then rinse with water.

Q: A few years ago we moved into a rented apartment with a light-beige carpeting that showed every spot. I bought a 9- by 12-foot rug to cover the living room and used double sticky tape to hold the rug in place. When I started to move and rearrange the rug, I found the sticky substance had transferred to the carpeting. Is there anything I can do to remove it, other than professional cleaning?

S. R., Manchester Center

A: We are assuming that your beige carpeting is nylon. The first thing you need is an over-the-counter rug-and-spot cleaner that contains a solvent (check the label). If you can't find one, buy some dry-cleaning solvent at your hardware store. After removing the adhesive, make up a solution of ½ teaspoon of nonbleaching powdered detergent to 1 pint water. Wash the spots with this and rinse with 1 tablespoon ammonia in 1 cup water. The rinse is *very* important, as the detergent, if left in the carpet, will act as a magnet and attract dust and lint.

SPILLED MILK

Q: Our son spilled a cup of milk on the carpet and didn't tell us until the following day. I tried cleaning it with ammonia and water, but the spot still smells of sour milk.

Turning Sour, Montpelier

A: Mix white vinegar and warm water in equal proportions and, using a circular motion, rub into the rug. Rinse with warm water. After the rug has dried, you may want to use a commercial rug freshener, but we doubt if this will be necessary.

MERCUROCHROME

Q: How can we remove the stains of Mercurochrome from our bathroom rug?

Anne Bixler, Pawlet

A: Mercurochrome is highly soluble in water: you should have drenched the spills right away and then mopped them up. But we know hindsight is not very helpful. We suggest you soak a rag with water and pour a liberal amount of baking soda on it, making a poultice. Lay the cloth, baking-soda-side down, on the rug overnight. Then, if it is an area rug, wash as usual; if wall-to-wall, scrub with warm water, using a circular motion.

Incidentally because Mercurochrome is water-based, it is virtually worthless as an antiseptic. As Frank, our pharmacist, noted: "Any effective antiseptic must have penetrating qualities—in other words, an ability to soak into the skin. Merthiolate, for instance, is effective because it contains alcohol. Put a drop of Mercurochrome on your skin, and it will just sit there. Merthiolate, on the other hand, will disappear almost immediately."

CHAPTER 4

LAUNDRY AND FABRIC CARE

When we began our column, there were no pre-laundry stain removers. With their invention, everything has changed—including the expense. Ivory soap (not expensive) rubbed into the fabric will do what pre-laundry stain removers will do, and cheaper. So will Lava on some stains, and Goop on others (but watch for color fastness). However, having everything in one bottle, and hang the expense, is admittedly so much more convenient!

In the early years, we received a ton of questions about polyester: removing stains and odors and keeping the polyester white. Dishwasher detergent is the ticket for the latter—we still get letters thanking us for that hint. Nowdays laundering must be easier, what with pre-laundry stain removers, cotton and poly-cotton blends—our laundry questions are few and far between.

ELECTRIC BLANKET

Q: I have an electric blanket I would like to have dry cleaned, but I haven't been able to locate a dry cleaner who will do it.

Ann Urwin, Fairhaven

A: No wonder! Dry-cleaning solvent would gobble up the insulation on the heating wires so that when you next plugged in the blanket you would have had the hottest coverlet in town. Wash your electric blanket in your washing machine using warm water and your favorite laundry detergent; then line dry.

BEDSPREAD

Q: I have an old, hand-crocheted bedspread which is very dirty. I don't want to harm it, as it is a family heirloom. Could you tell me how to wash it without harming it?

Beth Smith, Castleton

A: We assume the bedspread is cotton. If it is wool, the only difference from the following directions would be to use Woolite.

First, get someone to help you. Crochet is open-work and thus can stretch very easily. In washing and drying, therefore, it's important that you don't pull, twist or wring. Once the bedspread is wet, it should be washed by being lifted and turned from underneath. A bedspread is big and heavy, and one pair of arms is probably not enough.

Inspect the spread and do any necessary mending before you wash. Then fill a bathtub with lukewarm water and a mild detergent, and wash the spread. You may want to give it two or three changes of water if, as you say, it is very dirty.

Rinse well and gently press dry as you would a wool sweater, and dry flat. This probably means putting towels down on the floor of a room you don't use much and laying the bedspread out. Don't dry outside, as direct sunlight may cause it to turn yellow (if it is white) or fade (if it is dyed).

You may want to skip all of the above and have your bedspread dry cleaned instead, but a word of caution: discuss it with your dry cleaner first.

MATTRESS

Q: I would like to know how to get a urine spot (or whatever the stain is) from my new mattress. My grandson slept on it without a mattress pad. I found this big stain on it, so I hope you can help me in some way. Otherwise, my mattress is ruined. It was an expensive one.

E. C., Proctor

A: First wash the stain with cold water, then rub detergent into the stain and scrub with hot water and chlorine bleach. Rinse thoroughly. If the stain continues to be stubborn, sponge with straight white vinegar and rinse. This will not harm the mattress but may change the color of the fabric where you've cleaned it. You may want to wait for a sunny day to do this so you can take the mattress outside to dry and air.

FOAM RUBBER AND LATEX

Q: Any suggestions for cleaning a foam mattress used by an occasionally bedwetting child?

Curious in the Morning, Plainfield

A: We didn't have any practical suggestions for Curious, but Helen Wolfel, of Barre, wrote: "I deplore a dirty mattress, and our foam-rubber one always seemed dirtier after I'd cleaned it from a spill or an accident. I tried everything. Then my husband and I purchased a rug-cleaning vacuum cleaner from Sears which sucks up the liquid. It worked so well on rugs, I decided to use it on not only the foam mattress but all my other mattresses, which include foam-topped and spring-type. I used the floor attachment for the corners and sides. I use the Rinsenvac cleaning solution, which you can buy at hardware stores. I literally soak the mattress and then vacuum as much moisture as possible out of it. Then I lean the mattress on its side on top of a plastic sheet. I try to leave as much air circulating around the mattress as possible and let it stand with the hot sun directly on it. I usually turn the mattress on the second day so the sun shines on the other side. It's amazing how much dirt we sleep on and don't know it!"

Q: I have a latex foam pillow, and I was wondering how to wash it.

M. O., Ludlow

A: Remove the zippered cover, which you can toss into your washer and dryer. Launder the pillow by hand in warm water, using a mild detergent. To speed up the drying process, put the pillow between two towels and roll gently to squeeze out the excess moisture. Let dry at room temperature away from heating units and the sun.

FEATHERS

Q: I have some old feather pillows that have a very bad odor. What would be a good way to clean them? Must they be cleaned commercially, or is there an old remedy? I am almost tempted to wash them.

J. Billings, Ludlow

A: The old-fashioned remedy would have been to open the pillows, throw out the old feathers and restuff them with new ones. (We assume, by the way, that you have feather and not down pillows.) As most of us don't any longer have a supply of ducks or chickens in our back yard longing to give us their feathers, we suggest you put the pillows in a plastic garbage bag filled with deodorizing cat litter, seal tightly and leave for a week.

If that doesn't work you might try washing the pillows in lukewarm water with a mild detergent (dishwashing liquid would probably be the best) and then put them in the dryer with a sneaker (its buffeting around should help keep the feathers from matting). We don't promise great results either with dry cleaning or washing, as the quills, particularly if they are old and brittle, are likely to break, and the feathers, unlike down, will not hold their feather shape.

Our final suggestion is that you open the pillows, empty out the feathers and put them in a couple of pillow cases. Leave them out in the sun, shaking them around occasionally. Wash the pillow covers in your regular laundry and restuff.

COLOR FASTNESS

Q: I'm just back from a trip to Mexico and have brought back some hand-embroidered shirts and dresses. I am concerned that the bright colors of the embroidery will run when I wash these things. Is there anything I can do to set the color?

D. D., Chester

A: Before you launder your new Mexican clothes, soak them in a solution of 3 cups cold water, 1 cup vinegar and ¼ cup salt for a couple of hours. This solution will also guarantee color fastness in any cotton garment.

GORE-TEX

Q: I have a Gore-Tex jacket that needs washing. What's the best way to deal with it? Can I put it in the washer?

M. B., Barre

A: Do not dry clean Gore-Tex. Pop it in your washing machine, use cold water and a powdered detergent. Drip dry or tumble dry at a low setting.

SILK

Q: I'm tired of having to pay through the nose every time I have a silk blouse dry cleaned as per instructions on the label. Can I wash them?

E. L., Randolph

A: Wash your silk blouse in lukewarm water with Woolite. Squeeze gently and hang to dry. While it's still damp, roll the blouse up in a towel and put it in your freezer. When it has frozen really hard, remove it and iron on a low setting. Your blouse will come out looking absolutely brand new. Speaking of ironing, which neither of us get around to as often as we should, we have found the job is easier if you dampen your clothes, stick them in a plastic bag and store them for a while in the fridge. Even if the urge (or necessity) to iron doesn't hit you for months, your clothes will remain damp and mildewfree.

STORAGE

Q: I've been told that fur coats and jackets should not be stored in a cedar closet. True or false?

Marcy LaBonte, Cavendish

A: True. The best way to store fur is in cold storage, or if that is impossible, in a cool place where there is good air circulation. A cedar closet is a closed environment which will not give the fur a chance to "breathe" freely. With warm temperatures and inadequate circulation, the fur over time will become matted and flattened and the skins dry and brittle.

Q: I've been trying to find a place where I can purchase acid-free tissue paper. I have been carefully laundering a 140-year-old christening dress and petticoat. My grandfather wore it in 1847, and it has been worn by everyone in the family until now. Another grandchild is due in January. I have often read that wedding gowns, laces, etc., should be stored in acid-free tissue. No one I've asked has ever heard of it! If you have any information, I would appreciate it more than I can say. I am hoping the tradition will go on for another 140 years!

J. W., Montpelier

A: You are absolutely right: acid-free tissue paper is the conservator's wrapping of choice. You can order it through a catalogue issued by University Products, Inc., P.O. Box 101, Holyoke, MA 01401. The catalogue offers a full range of conservation supplies for museums, libraries and individuals. An item they stock which may be of particular interest to our readers wishing to preserve family papers and memorabilia is their Heritage Album. It contains (among other things) photo pages, binders for personal papers and see-through display sheets, all of which are acid-free.

DOWN

Q: I have a full-length down coat which I've owned for three years. The shell is made of a combination of polyester and nylon, and the lining is all nylon. After each wearing season I have it dry cleaned, according to instructions, before storing. My problem is, when I wear the coat and take it off, some of the down and small feathers make their way through the lining and stick to my clothes. The situation is worsened with static electricity. Is there anything I can do?

C. D., Montpelier

A: Our news for you isn't very encouraging. Regular dry-cleaning solvent is very harsh, and after a while will open up pores in the nylon, allowing space for down and small feathers to escape. A spokesperson for Eastern Mountain Sports, which makes a variety of down clothing, told us that contrary to instructions on the label, it's better for a down garment to be washed in a front-loading washing machine (i.e., one with a drum rather than an agitator) unless you can find a dry cleaner that specializes in down and uses a cleaning solvent called Stoddard. The companies making better-quality down garments are now putting a double liner on the inside of their products to lessen the chances of the lining becoming weakened and no longer "down proof."

Your only option is to spray the lining of your coat with Scotchguard, but this is a stopgap measure (so to speak) at best for, as you wear the coat, the Scotchguard will lose its effectiveness. There are also antistatic sprays on the market (in the supermarket laundry section, for instance) that will lessen, though not solve, your problem.

For readers who have a problem of down coats and vests shedding at the seams, we heartily recommend a product called Seam Sealer, made by Kenyon Company and available at most sporting-goods stores. It's viscous, like airplane glue, and is normally used to keep tents, tarps and sleeping bags from leaking. It's not very attractive looking, but as you'll only be using it on inside seams, it won't show.

ELASTIC REPLACEMENT

Q: Could you or one of your readers to tell me how to put new elastic on cotton underwear (ladies')? The undies are in good shape, but the elastic is all stretched out. I'd like to put new elastic on but am not sure how to.

V. E. D., Rutland

A: Our original answer turned out to be not very satisfactory: many of our frugal New England readers wrote to let us know that our solution was much more complicated than need be. M.P., of Graniteville, suggested that elastic lace be sewn right over the old elastic. Jean Stearns, of Springfield, also recommended elastic lace but suggested the old elastic be removed first. Our favorite solution came from Anna Pond, in Northfield: "I had the same problem; the old elastic stretched out and to put in new was a very trying job. So I bought some round white elastic, and using a darning needle that you sew yarn with, I ran the elastic right through the old stretched elastic. Then instead of trying to sew the round elastic, I just tied it into a good knot. It works like a charm and only takes about 10 minutes to do the job. I tried knotting in different places, and I find the side is best, but it really doesn't matter."

PERMANENT PRESS

Q: Would you tell me how to get stains out of a permanent press tablecloth; foodstains, and probably grease or oil?

Esther, Rutland

A: A friend of ours who owns a bed and breakfast establishment solved the problem, and although we've never come across this particular solution anywhere else, it works! Rub the spots with full-strength Lestoil, then machine wash with your usual detergent. The stains will be gone. Incidentally this trick will also re-move mildew from fabrics, but color test nonpermanent-press fab-rics for color fastness first.

KEEPING WHITES WHITE

Q: How do I keep white polyester blouses white without using bleach, which most washing directions forbid? Washing with Wool-ite doesn't seem to do the trick; they still tend to gray after a few washings.

A Rutland Reader

A: We have often extolled the many uses of automatic-dishwasher detergent and we still think it is one of the least utilized but best all-purpose cleaning agents around. Besides cutting grease, whisking away dirt (and cleaning your dishes) it also takes the gray, which is due to detergent residue build-up, out of white polyester.

Dissolve 1 cup of dishwasher detergent in 1 gallon of warm water. Soak your blouses in this mixture overnight, and the next morning run them through your washing machine. They will come out white and sparkling.

We don't recommend you do this every time you wash your blouses, as the dishwasher detergent contains lye and, with con-stant use, will shorten the life of the fabric.

RING AROUND THE COLLAR

Q: Thank you for your advice on getting rid of the gray. Dish-washer detergent works like a charm, but I still have "ring around the collar." Despite claims to the contrary, I haven't yet found a laundry detergent that works, even full strength.

R. L., Barre

A: The following trick works on all fabrics, not just polyester. Buy a bottle of the cheapest shampoo you can find, rub it into the collar with a generous hand, then wash in the machine as usual. The less expensive the shampoo, the more alkaline it is; the alkalinity dis-solves the body and hair oils that are holding in the grime.

PERSPIRATION

Q: Is there any way to remove the gummy yellow stain from garment underarms that comes from using certain deodorants? It not only is bad in polyester fabrics, it seems even worse in cotton and cotton blends.

Susan Beard, Rutland

A: The solution we originally published was somewhat complicated, involving two soakings with ammonia, then vinegar. E.B., of Rutland, sent us a simpler answer to the problem. "I find the best way to remove the yellow stain on garments is to wet the stained part and rub it well with a bar of Ivory soap (not flakes) and then rub vigorously with your hands. I find this treatment removes many stubborn stains, even grease from a pair of white gloves."

Q: One of our children has a problem with perspiration odor staying in clothes, even though the child takes daily baths and uses a stronger-than-average deodorant. Other children in the family don't have this problem. Is there some way to remove the odor from his clothes?

Perplexed Mother, Proctor

A: For nonsynthetic fabrics, dip the underarm area in water and then rub with a deodorant soap such as Dial. You can also add 1 cup of vinegar to the wash cycle in your machine. A reader suggested the following for both natural and wash-and-wear fabrics: "Start filling the tub of your washer with very hot water, add 1 to 1½ cups detergent and 1 cup liquid chlorine bleach. Wear rubber gloves and mix thoroughly with your hand until detergent is dissolved. Then add more hot or warm water as you wish. The bleach will remove the odor. If you are worried about using this method on finer garments, put a dollop of Lysol into a container with enough water to cover and soak the article for 10 minutes. Then wash as usual."

READER FEEDBACK: Two of our readers suggested Perplexed Mother's child's strong perspiration odor might be caused by a nutritional deficiency. Mrs. A. Cavallo said: "What the child should use is zinc. Farmers use it on their livestock both for decreasing odor and as an additional food supplement. I hope this info gets to the mother. She's working on a problem that doesn't have to exist."

Ruth Ogden, of Hartland, citing two books on "natural" nutrition, suggests dolomite tablets, which contain both magnesium and calcium. (A lack of magnesium can also cause body odor.) Foods high in zinc, she notes, are seafoods, nuts and seeds (sunflower and pumpkin especially). Also leafy vegetables, liver, mushrooms, wheat bran, wheat germ, brewer's yeast, onions, maple syrup and fertile eggs. Zinc is also helpful in the control of acne. White spots on the fingernails are indicative of lack of zinc. Chelated zinc tablets are available at health-food and drugstores, but we'd suggest consulting a doctor before taking any mineral supplements in tablet form.

PRESERVATION

Q: I have a sampler that was made in the early 1800s by someone in my family. Do you know somewhere I can get it cleaned? I don't want to do anything to harm it.

E. R., Barre

A: Please *don't* get it cleaned. The chances are that any attempt to clean it, no matter how careful or gentle, will damage it. Leave it as is and have it museum framed (i.e., backed with acid-free board and sealed against dust, dirt, etc.). The process is costly, but worth it.

Q: I hope you can help. I have an old tapestry, about five by six feet. I had it hanging on a wall, but it started to fray and I had to take it down. I would like to have it repaired and also rehang it properly. Can you suggest anyone?

Peggy Healey, Pittsfield

A: One of our best resources on conservation, as well as hard-to-find items in catalogues, is Meredith Wright, of Montpelier, who has recently started her own business after having consulted for museums for years. Called Heirloom Textile Conservation, she's specializing in consultation, restoration, cleaning and display of textiles and costumes. Her address is P.O. Box 686, Montpelier, VT 05602 (802-223-5753).

SHEDDING

Q: I have a 100-percent-acrylic scarf which sheds so badly that I am unable to wear it. Is there any way of finding something that will rectify this problem for me so that I can enjoy this very pretty scarf?

Phyllis Wilder, Rutland

A: Hand wash and rinse your scarf in warm water, then spin it in the washing machine and lay it over a rack to dry. Spinning it to get out the excess moisture will also help to felt or mat the fibers together and should stop the shedding.

Q: Recently I purchased a sweater made of 48-percent silk, 30-percent nylon, 10-percent angora rabbit hair and 2-percent lamb's wool. It is a beautiful sweater but it sheds. I was told to put it in a plastic bag and place it in the freezer for a couple of days, which I did, but it still sheds. Do you have any ideas?

J. H., Wallingford

A: It is the angora, which is fur rather than wool, that is the culprit. It is an inescapable fact that hair, unlike wool, sheds. If you look closely at a strand of wool you will see that it has interlocking fibers, whereas hair grows as smooth as a strand of thread. We have a friend who knitted a sweater from "wool" spun from the hair of her husband's beloved dog. "He walks around," she noted, "in a haze of floating dog fur."

We aren't surprised that the freezer trick didn't work. As soon as the sweater begins to thaw it naturally starts shedding again.

We suggest you spray your sweater lightly with Static Guard. Electricity in the air will cause the sweater to shed more than it normally would. If you have a house cat, you've probably noticed that it sheds more in the winter. This is in large part caused by low humidity in the air and a resulting increase in static electricity. Good luck. And by the way, mohair does the same thing.

SOFT LEATHER

Q: I have a pair of beige deerskin gloves that have become very soiled. How do I clean them?

Anna Symes, Hydeville

A: Most deerskin gloves are hand washable unless they are lined: then they should be dry cleaned. Put them on your hands and make a heavy lather with a little warm water and pure soap, such as Ivory. Rinse with a somewhat lighter lather. Do not use plain water. Roll the gloves up in a towel and dry away from any heat. If the leather is too stiff when dry, the rinsing lather was too thin. Correct by rewetting in heavier soapsuds. For larger pieces of soft leather, such as coats or skirts, rub in the lather and scrape off until the lather comes clean. Rinse and dry as above.

SHEEPSKIN

Q: I am writing to find out a way to thoroughly clean a sheepskin so the skin side stays soft and pliable. A lady who raises sheep and sells skins, who should know, told me to just throw it into the washer with Ivory Flakes and then in the dryer. She said it was perfectly safe and would in no way dry out the skin. Well, she was wrong. (You can do this with treated skins sold in medical supply and other stores as long as the package label says the skin has been treated.) So now what?

Leslie Van Ness, Rutland

A: The following method is absolutely fool-proof, we promise. Wash your sheepskin in the washing machine on Gentle cycle with cold water and Woolite. During the Rinse cycle, also on cold, add ¼ cup hair conditioner or creme rinse. This serves to condition the skin and make it soft and pliable. In dryer set on Fluff (coolest temperature) dry the skin, but be careful not to overdry. Take out immediately and brush with whichever brush is handy.

SNEAKERS AND RUNNING SHOES

Q: I have three pairs of Nikes, different colors, so very comfortable that I now dislike wearing real shoes. How do you clean them? I've tried soap and water, Comet and Top Job, but they make no impression. I haven't put my Nikes in the washing machine, as I don't know if they would survive, and I'd rather have dirty ones than battered and raggedy ones. Can you suggest a cleansing bath for these so-very-comfortable foot-easers?

Louise Morse, Williamstown

A: We assume, as you do, that any shoe that is leather or has leather trim should never be machine washed. For future reference the best way to maintain your running shoes is to clean them as soon as they get dirty; the nylon and mesh are so tightly woven that if dirt isn't removed pronto it becomes increasingly difficult to get out. The most effective tool for cleaning your running shoes is soap and water applied with an old toothbrush. Any kind of soap will do. Our source for the answer to your question also noted that any time a leather or leather-trimmed shoe gets wet or is shampooed, it should be stuffed with newspaper and allowed to air dry.

READER FEEDBACK: One of our readers wrote to let us know that we (and our source, who should have known better, as he owns a sports store) were wrong on almost all counts above. Vinnie wrote,

"I was told not to wash my Nikes in the washing machine, but I did anyway. I put them right in with my washing and they came out beautiful. I don't put them in the dryer, but I don't stuff them with newspapers, either, as it smudges them." An anonymous gentleman wrote that the toothbrush method should be used with Octagon, Ivory Liquid or some other dishwashing detergent. "A bit of water with it is okay. A couple of tablespoons of the same detergent and warm water is also excellent for washing sweaters, even cashmere. Measure the sweaters before washing, stretch them to size and dry on a large beach towel."

GRASS STAINS

Q: How do you remove grass stains from children's baseball uniforms?

M. Ryan, White River Junction

A: We gave yet another lengthy answer that we'd gleaned from the pages of our government-issue stain-removal pamphlet: there were about 20 steps and 10 strange ingredients (like amyl acetate and banana oil) involved. We asked our readers for better ideas and got them! Two readers suggested washing with Lestoil, another said Lava soap, rubbed briskly into the stains, would take them right out. B.R., of Wells River, said, "For grass or blood stains rub Ivory or other white cake soap into stain and let stand 20 minutes. Rinse in tepid water." Finally, "Grammy," in Fair Haven, wrote: "Try Goop Hand Cleaner, available at your grocery store. It's a multipurpose cleaner and works on all my grass stains." This was the first we'd heard of Goop, which has taken its place with vinegar, dishwasher detergent, baking soda and denture cleanser as a favorite household product. It removes pet stains from rugs and gum from animal and human hair. It takes out perspiration stains—you name it!

For example. . . .

Q: How do you get latex paint out of clothing?

Harold Adome, Brandon

A: Goop!

STAINS FROM WHITES

Q: My husband spilled spaghetti sauce on a brand-new pair of white cotton trousers, and I can't get the stain out. Suggestions, please!

S. R., Berlin

A: Once again we were saved by reader feedback. Jane Kababik, of Brandon, suggested spraying the spot with Tilex Bathroom Cleaner and immediately putting the trousers in the wash. (She cautions *not* to use Tilex on colored or synthetic fabrics.) Fran Setien, of Barre, says, "She might try Rit Rust Remover. I bought some as a last resort for some white culottes ruined by spaghetti sauce. Nothing else worked, but this made the garment look like new!"

INK

Q: I work for an inn in the laundry. The trouble I'm having is in removing ink spots, large and small, from white cotton-polyester shirts. The woman who sold the shirts to the inn recommended hair spray, but it doesn't do the trick.

Carol M. Eaton, Rutland

A: Try straight rubbing alcohol: it will take ball-point ink out of almost anything washable.

IRON AND RUST

Q: I have some white pillowcases that have turned orange-yellow from the iron in our well water. I've tried bleach and water, but it just makes it worse. Is there anything I can do to whiten them?

B. M. K., White River Junction

A: You can try Rit Rust Remover (available at big supermarkets, fabric and discount stores) or the old-fashioned recipe of water and cream of tartar. Add 4 tablespoons cream of tartar to each pint of water, bring to a boil and put your pillowcases in the boiling solution until they come white. Another old-timer is to mix oxalic acid crystals (available from your pharmacist) in cold water: dip pillowcases in and out of the solution until the discoloration has disappeared. Rinse immediately in a bath of cold water to keep the fabric from being harmed.

FRUIT

Q: Can you tell me how to remove peach, cherry or plum juice from clothing? I've tried several things, and the stain still remains.
Theresa Nadler, West Rutland

A: Boiling water works best. Put on your kettle, stretch the stained parts of the garment over a pot or bowl, pour the boiling water over the stain and it will disappear. We have also found when cutting up cherries and plums that rubbing a cut lemon on stained fingers and hands will remove the stains quick as a wink. If the boiling-water method doesn't work for you, try lemon juice and water.

SHRUNKEN SWEATER

Q: I have a new sweater that is 50-percent lamb's wool and 50-percent angora. It was accidently put in the washer and is now half its original size. Is there anything I can do?
K. Bride, Rutland

A: We hate to tell you this, but as far as we know, there isn't anything you can do. Wool fibers have small hooklike hairs along their length. When exposed to heat these hairs pull tightly together—and that's that. It's this interlocking activity that makes wool so much warmer than acrylic or cotton, both of which have smooth fibers (that's why they stretch). Wool, treated properly, will hold its shape. We've heard of soaking shrunken wool sweaters in fabric softener, but it's never worked for us.

READER FEEDBACK: Berenicia Law, of Danville, suggests washing the shrunken sweater in shampoo. "I know by experience this works on other sweaters, but I'm not sure about wool." This made us wonder whether washing in a hair conditioner might unlock the fibers. If the shrunken sweater is useless as is, it would be worth a try.

WAX STAIN

Q: After a wedding at our old church we found candles had melted on the pulpit, which is covered with a material that has a nap. How do we remove the tallow?

Madeline Slack, Corinth

A: Your best bet is first, using a fingernail brush, to get as much of the excess wax off as possible. Then cover the area with a piece of blotting paper and go over it slowly with an iron set at medium heat.

WRINKLES, NO-IRON AND IRONS

Q: I recently washed a pair of my husband's permanent-press slacks. When I removed them from the washer they were badly wrinkled, and after another rinse the wrinkles remain. The same thing happened to a blouse last summer. Any suggestions?

Ruth Ann Carey, Wallingford

A: We hope that you have a dryer, because this works for us. Toss the wrinkled permanent-press duds into the dryer with a wet towel, set at medium heat and in 10 minutes they should be wrinkle-free.

Q: Can you tell me how to best remove creases from a flannel-backed vinyl tablecloth? The instructions say no ironing.
V. N. Baskevitch, Springfield

A: If you have a clothes dryer, pop your tablecloth in at a low setting for a few minutes. The other method, despite the no-iron instructions, is to iron the tablecloth, flannel side up, at a low setting.

Q: Can you give me any suggestions as to how to take out wrinkles in my new Skirt-It? It's plastic, and I've tried dipping it in the bathtub in warm water and letting it drip dry, but that didn't help much.
W. E., Pittsford

A: The water must be hot enough to make the plastic limp: try a good hot-water soak and then drip dry.

Q: Each time I buy an iron, I use it for a short while, and then it starts to spit and leak on the steam setting. I wrote to the company, and they told me to take it to an appliance service center. The center charges $25 just to look at the iron. I even use distilled water in it, to no avail. Is there some way to prevent this happening again when I buy a new iron? Or is it possible to cure the one I have?
J. G., Chittenden

A: Bill, our good friend and endless fount of information at the Authorized Appliance Service Center, in Rutland, was horrified that you would be charged $25 just to look at the iron. He considered that to be highway robbery, as most irons don't even cost that much in the first place. He went on to tell us that there are three possible causes of your problem. First, your cord may have become damaged in some way so that the amount of electricity running into your iron fluctuates, causing a like fluctuation of temperature in the coil that turns the water to steam. As the cord is heavily covered with insulating material, this damage may not be visible.
    Second, the iron's thermostat may be defective.
    Third, and most likely, is that you didn't use distilled water from the very first use of the iron. Minerals from your water built up, plugging the vents. If that is the case, he advises that you pour

straight white vinegar into the iron and turn it on to the steam setting. If you can, set the iron outside during this process as it will smell terrible and, if inhaled, the evaporating vinegar will cause a burning sensation in your nose and throat. Keep the iron on until the vinegar is gone, then rinse out with water. This should do the trick, but there is also a chance that the vinegar will loosen the sediment and cause the iron to become totally and irretrievably blocked. Bill says it's a chance you'll have to take, though it only happens about 20 percent of the time.

Bill noted that irons, if used on a regular basis, only last two or three years nowadays. Finally, we asked him about the warning that came with our iron that said, "Do not use distilled water." He laughed.

CHAPTER 5

FURNITURE
FIX-UP

Furnishing our houses is an on-going project. Our homes are loaded with furniture that could best be described as "early attic"—comfy couches whose springs rest on the floor, easy chairs that once graced our parents' living rooms, wedding-present lamps and oriental rugs sporting worn-through spots. Clutter abounds in both our houses and is added to when we go yard sailing. We, like many of our readers, are more interested in repairing and reviving the old than in buying the new.

CHIPPED ENAMEL

Q: I have an old Hoosier kitchen cabinet which needs repair work on the slide-out shelf. It's made of enamel and has some chips. Can anyone repair this?

Norma Raymond, East Montpelier

A: You can repair the chips with a product called Duro White Appliance Touch-Up. We found it at our hardware store. It's for repairing nicks and scratches on enamel and porcelain surfaces.

CRIBS

Q: I have two cribs that have been sitting on the floor in a basement room for 20 years. The room is damp, dirty, musty and mildewy. Crib 1 is 22 years old. Its paint (stain and varnish) is okay, but it smells musty. Crib 2 is 60 years old with a couple of layers of paint that is chipping. Its musty odor is bad. How can I restore these cribs so they can be used safely again?

M. S., Springfield

A: Maybe you shouldn't try. Old cribs have been found to be hazardous because of their lack of safety features. One problem is that there is often too much space between crib slats. This poses a great danger for infants, as they can get their heads stuck between them. Ideally slats should not be more than 2⅜ inches apart. Babies can also get hung up on the posts or finials at the corners of the crib. Sharp metal fittings are also dangerous. In addition paint that is more than 25 years old should be stripped off. Chances are it's lead based and very poisonous. These are just a few of the problems with old cribs. We suggest that you write for a free copy of "Crib Safety: Keep Them on the Safe Side," Product Safety Fact Sheet No. 43, from the U.S. Consumer Product Safety Commission, Washington, DC 20207.

To get rid of the mold and mildew put the crib in the sun. Wash it down with a solution of half ammonia and half water, and if that doesn't do the trick wash again with full-strength Lysol. Be sure and give it a good sun bath. If the crib rails have been chewed you can buy a new pair of "teething rails" which are plastic and snap onto the crib rails.

LOOSE CHAIR RUNGS

Q: I'm having difficulty regluing a chair, and I hope you can help. The holes where the rungs fit are so worn that glue won't hold them; they wobble around. What can I do?

Glue Won't Do, St. Johnsbury

A: We have two solutions to offer you. The first is: cut a piece of fabric from an old nylon stocking or a pair of panty hose. Put some glue on the rung and stretch the piece of nylon over it. Apply more glue and fit the rung into the hole. When the glue (we assume you're using a good wood glue) has dried, trim the nylon sticking out of the hole with a razor blade. Or buy a product called Chair-Loc, which is made by a company of the same name in Lakehurst, New Jersey. It's not a glue but a product which penetrates the wood fibers and actually swells the wood to tighten the joints.

ACCIDENTALLY IMPRINTED UPHOLSTERY

Q: Recently a guest of ours lay on our sofa with a heating pad under her. The sofa is upholstered with a velvet material, and the heating pad left its imprint on the cushion. It's as if someone used a hot iron on it. Can anything be done to raise the imprint?

D. N., Rutland

A: It seems odd to suggest you use a hot iron to get rid of this particular imprint, but that's what we're going to do. First, lay a piece of woolen fabric over the spot, and on top of that a piece of dampened muslin. Go back and forth over the muslin with an iron, with the setting betwen Cotton and Linen. The wool will protect the velvet, while the steam from the muslin, passing through the wool, will soften the crushed nap of the velvet. Finally, remove the cloths, and carefully brush up the nap with a toothbrush.

STICKY CHAIR ARMS AND FURNITURE POLISH

Q: What can be used on wooden dining-room chair arms (antique and reproduction) that have a sticky build-up from wiping hands on the arms? What is recommended for polishing furniture, mainly tables: oil, wax or cream polish?

Constance B. Woolson, Springfield

A: To find the answers to your questions we went right to the top and visited Jonathan Schectman, founder of Preservation Consulting Services, in Quechee. Besides being an antiquarian and historian, Jonathan has studied furniture restoration both here and in England. In answer to your first question, he recommends two things.

First make a mild solution of warm water and dish detergent and wash the arms. If that doesn't get rid of the stickiness use the following formula, which comes from an English cabinetmaker with whom Jonathan worked. He calls it Salad Oil.

> 1 part white distilled vinegar
> 1 part raw linseed oil
> 1 part paint thinner
> 1 part denatured alcohol

Place in a bottle and shake vigorously. Now decant some into a container and have a third container ready. With some Number-0000 steel wool, take some of the solution from the second container and, going with the grain, clean gently. Every third stroke or so, squeeze off the steel wool into the third container. If the mixture doesn't seem to be working, add a little more alcohol to the second container. Jonathan warned that it's important to be very careful not to damage the original finish. That is, don't mistake dirt for veneer.

As to your second question, the first thing to do is remove all the old polish and wax. Do this by rubbing the surface with a detergent-and-water solution. Then take a cloth saturated with paint thinner and rub with the grain. For a finishing polish, Jonathan Schectman recommends Renaissance, a microcrystalline wax that is made in England and does not streak or discolor. It's completely pure and is also long-lasting both in the jar and on the surface. It's very expensive and available from Brookstone in Peterborough, New Hampshire. A locally available product Jonathan recommends is Trewax.

READER FEEDBACK: Mrs. J.A. Read, from Brandon, wrote, "Paint thinner and steel wool can do more damage than good if used by the inexperienced. I used Scott's Liquid Gold on my gummy dining-room chairs, and lo and behold, they have a lovely light finish and come clean with very little trouble."

Removing White Rings on Table

Q: I have an old coffee table made of wood which has a hand finish on it. A guest recently placed a hot, drippy mug of tea on the table leaving a white ring. I normally clean the table with Weiman's Furniture Cream, as lemon oil doesn't penetrate. I tried mayonnaise to rid the table of its mark, but it didn't correct the problem. I would really like to avoid having it refinished, so I would greatly appreciate a solution.

Chris Atkin, Montpelier

A: Take some cigar or cigarette ash and rub the ring using a cloth dipped in lubricating, vegetable or salad oil. Wipe immediately and put some of your furniture polish on.

READER FEEDBACK: To remove white rings and spots from furniture rub with camphorated oil and immediately rub with any furniture polish.

To remove white water stains from a Danish walnut table place some rottenstone powder (available at paint or hardware stores)— or cigar ashes if no rottenstone is available—in a shallow dish. Soak felt pad in camphorated oil; a piece of old felt hat is ideal. Squeeze excess oil from felt leaving felt thoroughly soaked. Press wet felt into rottenstone, and working with the grain rub the spot. Continue until the spot disappears.

George D. Farwell makes stain remover that he sells at craft fairs and through the mail. He wrote, "We have been in business for over 40 years. One of our products is Santash, a liquid that removes white or milky stains from wood, trays and other pieces. The recipe you gave for people to make themselves will remove the stain, but the compound you recommend will also scratch the surface of the finished piece of furniture or a painted tray. Santash has a special ingredient that does a marvelous job without blemishing the finish in any way." Santash is available through The Shop of William Farwell, 140 Holly St., Rutland, VT 05701.

DIRTY LEATHER IN COFFEE TABLE

Q: I have what I believe is a Duncan Phyfe coffee table which has two squares of burgundy leather edged in gold. My problem is that the leather has dirt in the grooves which I can't get out. I have tried saddle soap and oil soap, but they never seem to do the trick. Do you have any recommendations?

T. G., Montpelier

A: If you've waxed or polished the table with frequency the grooves have probably accumulated a build-up of wax, polish and dust that can't be removed with soap. Clean the grooves with 100-percent mineral-spirits paint thinner, wash with saddle soap, and polish with any neutral shoe polish.

DIRTY REED CHAIR BACKS

Q: I have kitchen chairs with double reed backs. I have never found anything advertised for cleaning reed. I hope you can help.

D. M. P., Springfield

A: The first thing to do is to vacuum the chairs with a brush attachment. Then make up a very mild solution of warm water and dishwashing liquid and wash the reed using a fine nylon brush. We don't know if the reed on your chairs is covered with varnish or shellac, but if so don't soak the reed. Be sure to dry the reed thoroughly with rags or bath towels. If the reed is varnished and it's wearing down, consider replacing it.

STORING FURNITURE

Q: Within a few months, I'm going to store my furniture in an unheated shed. I'm worried that my furniture, which is solid oak, will be ruined. Please give me some suggestions on making sure that it will be in good shape after five years.

K. C., Ludlow

A: We called on the expertise of Hank and Mimi Savelberg, manufacturers of fine oak furniture, in Hartland. They said, "Don't do it." Wood naturally expands and contracts and the extremes of temperature we get here, plus inevitable dampness, will almost certainly cause your furniture to warp and crack. They recommed you spend whatever extra it will cost to store your furniture with an insured storage company. Solid-oak furniture would be very expensive to replace and/or repair.

WICKER REFINISHING

Q: I have an old wicker rocker which we use on the patio in the summer. It probably has a trillion coats of paint on it and has dried out considerably. Can it be restored to a natural finish? How do I go about doing that? And what could I do to keep it from becoming brittle?

Linda Mattson, Rutland

A: The only way to get paint off wicker is to take it to a furniture stripper who dips. Even so, if your chair is fiber rush rather than rattan or cane you are out of luck, as it won't withstand the dipping process. You can easily identify fiber-rush wicker, as it is always round, while rattan and cane wicker are $1/2$-inch oval or flat. Fiber rush is actually ground Kraft paper that has been twisted into long strands. Once your chair has been dipped, you'll probably want to spray paint it, for even after the dipping there will still be little freckles and specks of old paint remaining beween the interweavings of the wicker. Use a latex spray paint rather than an enamel, which forms a hard, impermeable surface. The way to keep your wicker from becoming brittle in the first place is to hose it down with spray mist from your hose two or three times a summer.

CHAPTER 6

REPAIRS OF ALL SORTS

Vermonters subscribe to the "use it up, wear it out, get it fixed or do without" school of thought. Our readers are one of our best resources, and if we can't answer a question they almost always do. We dedicate this chapter to all the Mr., Mrs., Miss and Ms. Fixits.

BOOK BINDINGS

Q: I have two old English history books badly in need of repair. The bindings are not leather, and the books have value only to the family. If you could give me a line on whom to see about their repair, I would be most grateful.

L. M., Montpelier

A: Restoring your books is costly. A book is grouped into "signatures" which are sewn-together sections that usually contain from 10 to 20 pages. When a book starts to "shake" (i.e., the signature pages come loose from the bindings) the entire book has to be resewn with needle and thread, then reglued to the spine (the binding between the two covers). All this has to be done by hand and so is apt to cost a bare minimum of $50 per book. Rare and/or antiquarian book dealers are great resources, as they generally know who the best book binders are. Check your Yellow Pages for one near you. Our resource is the Antiquarian Bookseller in North Pomfret.

BROKEN BIRD BATH

Q: Do you know how to repair a broken bird bath?

Eleanor Rider, Castleton

A: If your bird bath is made of concrete and is broken in half there is no way of repairing it. If the damage is just a crack or a "plug" that has popped out, however, you can buy a hydraulic cement called Easy Plug that expands as it hardens. You can find it at building-supply stores or a concrete-block plant.

CROCK

Q: I have an old 15-gallon crock which has been deteriorating badly, I assume from a brine put in it many years ago. The surface has been flaking off, both the outside white and the inside brown glaze. Is there any way to prevent this from continuing, and if so, is there any method to restore damaged areas?

R. E. I., Poultney

A: Unfortunately it's too late to do anything to save the crock. Salt from the brine has penetrated the glaze and entered the crockery, and there is no way to remove it. Salt attracts and holds moisture, thereby making the clay, of which the crock is made, expand. That is what caused the flaking to occur.

CRYSTAL

Q: I have a Waterford crystal bowl that has a small nick on the edge. Can I do anything to smooth it out?

Reader, Rutland

A: You can use either some very fine sandpaper or the finer grained side of any emery board. Smooth gently from the edges of the nick toward the center. It will take a while, but your patience will eventually be rewarded by a nick-free bowl.

DOLLS

Q: I have a doll that was mine in the early 1920s. She is good-sized, about two feet tall with a china face and eyes that open and close. Her hair appears to be real. The problem is that she needs restringing, as she seems to be held together with two bands of some kind of rather thick, stretchy material which has deteriorated. My intention is to give her to my granddaughter as a keepsake. Do you know of anyone who can refurbish older dolls?

Loraine Reed, North Clarendon

A: A resource for doll parts is Doll Parts Supply Co., Inc., 46-50 54th Ave., Masbeth, NY 11378 (800-336-DOLL). They have a huge inventory of doll parts and accessories, not all of which are listed in their catalogue. If they don't have what you want in stock, they may be able to tell you who does. Doll bodies are available through the TDI Co., 6820 East Cave Creek Rd., Cave Creek, AZ 85331.

BOTCHED GLUE JOB

Q: We have a porcelain lamp base which fell and broke. With the aid of Borden's Elmer's Epoxy Cement I have glued it together, but in the time between the application of the cement and the drying two pieces shifted so that the rest of the pieces do not fit together. I have tried to cut the pieces that shifted apart but have not been successful. I have inquired at local hardware stores to find a way of separating the pieces but have found no help, or anyway none that worked. Do you know of any means to loosen the glue between the pieces that have shifted?

B. J. B., Rutland

A: A jeweler, who happens to be one of our faithful readers, told us he uses Elmer's Epoxy Bond Glue to set stones in settings. "When I've made a mistake, I just dip the whole thing into liquid Zip-Strip for 24 hours or as long as it takes to break the seal. Then I use a toothpick to scrape off any residue." He saw no reason why it would harm porcelain as long as there was no painting over the glaze.

CRACKED LAMP BASE

Q: We have an old table lamp that has been in the family for several generations. It stands about 24 inches tall with a bronzelike base and a 20-inch metal-and-glass shade. It is in good condition except that over the years the tapered top of the base has cracked and sagged inward on one side. Even so, it is quite sturdy. Can such damage be repaired and, if so, do you know someone who can do it?

Wallace Elton, Springfield

A: The metal base of your lamp is probably a mixture of tin, antimony and copper—i.e., an alloyed metal commonly known as "pot tin." (If your lamp base is over 100 years old, it probably also contains lead.) It's difficult to solder these older alloys because each maker used a different formula, and figuring out the solder that will best do the job is a complicated process. Local antique dealers, libraries and craft centers are great resources when it comes to finding repair people.

STUCK-TOGETHER STAMP COLLECTION

Q: While I lived abroad for 12 years, my postage-stamp collection remained in this country and was stored in a location which was, unfortunately, often damp! Most of the collection's uncanceled plate blocks and unused single stamps are firmly stuck to each other, in some instances mounted. Can you advise me how to get these stamps loose without damaging the adhesive and the face of the stamp? There are over 200 of the plate blocks.

Ken Gibson, Dorset

A: Phil Elwert, curator of the Vermont Historical Society, suggested that freeze-drying the stamps might be a way to unstick them. "Recently, this process of food preservation has been used to salvage water-soaked books, maps, furs, computer parts and other articles. John A. McGill of American Freeze-Dry Inc. in New Jersey (609-546-0777) will be able to advise Mr. Gibson if this process has application," he wrote.

READER FEEDBACK: C.W. Tucker, of Graniteville, suggested a steaming procedure to unstick the stamps. Since the value of stamps is reduced by at least half if the adhesive is gone, he also thought some of the adhesive might be saved if the stamps were put in a "moisture" chamber. He suggested putting a warm, wet but squeezed-out terry towel in the bottom of a roasting pan. Then put in a rack with a piece of cardboard on top of it. Put one plate block on top of this and put the lid on the pan. Check after a few hours to see if the stamps are loosening. If they are take them apart with stamp tongs and put them glue side down on a piece of window glass to dry. The glue might be partially left on.

SHEEN LOSS IN STERLING SILVER

Q: I accidentally put a sterling silver cup in an inch or two of Clorox. Where the silver met the Clorox, the cup lost its sheen. Nothing I've tried—including silver polish, of course—seems to restore it. Any suggestions?

Ellen Cole, Plainfield

A: What's happened is that your cup was in the Clorox long enough to etch the metal. Our recommendation is that you take the cup to a jeweler and have it repolished. Since it's sterling it will come back to its previous shine.

UMBRELLAS

Q: Can you tell me where I can have an umbrella repaired?
R. J., Waitsfield

A: Umbrellas seem to have joined the list of disposables and as a result, umbrella repair shops are scarce as hen's teeth. However, we found one near Boston: Essex Umbrella Mfg., 145 Old Colony Ave., Quincy, MA 02169 (617-770-2707).

TIMEX REPAIRS

Q: Do you know of anyone who can repair Timex wrist watches? The Timex Corporation will send a new watch in exchange for an old one for the price of the repair job. For sentimental reasons I want to keep my Timex wind-up watches, which I prefer to the quartz.
Ella Ward, Plymouth

A: We spoke with someone in customer service at Timex. She said that after sending a watch to Timex for repair, an invoice for the cost of the repair is sent back to the customer, who pays Timex. Timex either sends back the repaired watch, or if the repairs are impossible (or too expensive), they send a replacement. If you *don't want* a replacement, write on your return invoice "Please Do Not Replace But Repair." If they can't repair your watch they'll send it and your money back. If you are sending your watch by mail send it to Timex Corp., P.O. Box 2740, Little Rock, AR 72203. If you prefer using UPS, the address is Timex, Building 19, Adams Field, Little Rock, AR 72203. The Tick-Tock Shop in Burlington also repairs Timex watches. Just mail yours to 185 Bank St., Burlington, VT 05401, and they'll fix them for you.

CHAPTER 7

DOING IT YOURSELF

We live in old houses—Anne's is 200 and Nan's is 90. We will never know what it feels like to have everything that needs to be repaired, repaired, or everything that needs paint, painted, or furniture and floors all refinished.

We're lucky. Our houses have cozy window seats, nooks and crannies perfect for hide and seek, a ramble of rooms ideal for parties or privacy. We are blessed with greenhouses that warm our bodies and our spirits. Living in an old house is not a losing battle but a lifelong project.

CHIMNEY PROBLEMS

Q: I would appreciate any help you can give in solving a chimney problem. In an effort to blend in with an old cottage, we used very old bricks for a chimney. We now find that after a rain these old bricks are so porous they absorb water and that the moisture penetrates the wall of that part of the cottage exposed to the chimney. Have you any suggestion as to what we might use for a permanent sealer to remedy this situation? We would like to keep the old-brick look.

R. M. E., Montpelier

A: A clear masonry silicone sealer is the solution to your problem. Clean the brick with a fairly soft scrub brush. Then apply a silicone sealer such as Tru-Test, which is a 5-percent silicone resin in a paint thinner.

Q: What can be done to stop wallpaper from curling and cracking in corners, especially around chimneys? Somewhere I have an answer to this problem, but nothing I've tried works. I hope you will be able to answer this for me, as I papered my kitchen, and the paper curled up. I need to paper my dining room and do not want the same thing to happen.

B. H. Dennis, Rutland

A: There is unfortunately very little you can do about the peeling and cracking that has already occurred except to repaste the paper and paint it over with a thin coat of clear shellac. Use caution in doing this around chimneys, however, as some shellac is very flammable. Read the label.

For your new papering job, make sure the surfaces of the walls are properly prepared. First remove all the old wallpaper (soaking the walls with a paint roller dipped in hot water will do the trick nicely). Then paint the walls with an oil-based primer/sealer and follow that with a coat of sizing. (These products are available in any paint and wallpaper store.) As you've had trouble with wallpaper peeling and cracking, our expert suggests that you not use pre-pasted wallpaper, but purchase a vinyl-type paste that will contract and expand with the paper. Finally, use a vinyl seam adhesive on all the edges.

READER FEEDBACK: Mrs. Brault, of Barre, wrote to suggest that a way to solve this problem is to glue a strip of old cotton sheet on the corner or around the chimney and then glue the paper on top. "I have seen it work—try it," she said.

CLOCK HAND'S REPAIR

Q: I have a Black Forest Cuckoo Clock that was sent to me shortly after World War II from Germany. It keeps good time, and we like the cuckoo on the hour and the half-hour. Unfortunately the large hand has broken off. I've tried every way I know to put it back together again, but with no luck. Where can I get new hands?

E. Elmer, Brandon

A: There is a company called Klock-It that carries all kinds of clock faces, numerals, hands and electric and wind-up clock mechanisms. You can send for their free catalogue by writing the firm at P.O. Box 629, Highway H North, Lake Geneva, WI 55147.

CRACKS IN HARDWOOD FLOOR

Q: We cut cherry and maple logs from our land and took them to the mill to be tongue-and-grooved and made into 3-inch-wide boards for flooring. By mistake they were cut into 3-inch, 4-inch and 6-inch boards. We let them dry nine months, and they warped and were real hard to fit into the grooves when we laid the floor. Consequently we have up to ¼-inch cracks in a lot of places where the boards should meet. Our question is, what substance can we use to fill the worst of the cracks before we revarnish the floor? We tried wood putty last year, but it just dries up and falls out. We will be ready to refinish the floor again this spring and would like some ideas as to what we can do.

David and Suzanne Dessureau, Washington

A: A restoration expert tells us you have two options. The first is to cut tiny strips of wood and glue them between the cracks with a good white glue such as Titebond. This is a lot of work. The second option, and one that he has used with great success, is to buy a product called WoodEpox, which is made by Abatron, Inc. You actually fill the cracks with it, and it's very important that you scrape out the cracks thoroughly so the WoodEpox can bond. It doesn't flake or chip, and it accepts stain. Our expert also suggest that you buy a solvent from the same firm called Absolv. When you apply the WoodEpox you can drag it with a putty knife and wipe the knife with Absolv, which will eliminate tons of sanding. Abatron also makes a LiquidWood and Abocrete for repairing concrete permanently. For more information on these products or their application you can write the company 141 Center Drive, Gilberts, IL 60136, and they'll respond within five days, or you can call them at 312-426-2200 for an immediate answer.

FURNITURE PLANS

Q: My husband and I are interested in a bed for our son that looks like a car. The prices for these are very high. Where can we find plans for these types of children's twin beds?

C. J. F., West Rutland

A: For a pattern for a bed that looks like a Trans Am racing car send $4.50 to Grit Projects, P.O. Box 2383, Van Nuys, CA 91409-2383, and ask for Bedmobile No. 502.

Q: I've been looking everywhere for a set of plans for a wide-arm wooden armchair, at one time called an "Adirondack" chair. Do you know where I could find some?

R. G., Montpelier

A: Many lumberyards carry Easi-Bild Patterns of all kinds: furniture, lawn ornaments, bird houses, etc. If you can't find the patterns, write the firm at Easi-Bild Pattern Co., Box 2383-15241, Pleasantville, NY 10570. Plans are advertised in magazines such as *Popular Mechanics*, *Workbench* and *Craftsmen*.

KITCHEN CUPBOARD FINISH

Q: My kitchen cupboards are oiled-walnut veneer. Is it possible to use a polyurethane finish on the wood after oil has been used on it?

A Reader, Springfield

A: Our paint expert said that if the oil has soaked in—that is, if it hasn't recently been applied—you can put polyurethane finish on your cupboards. First wash them thoroughly to remove finger-prints and oil from people's hands. He suggested you do a test patch to make sure the oil won't be a problem. If the test areas dry thoroughly, go ahead with the new finish.

PAINT OVER VARNISH

Q: The glassed-in breezeway of our house has two doors and wooden trim that were painted some years back. At least two coats of varnish have been put over the paint. We wish to paint over that and would like to know how best to proceed.

Dora Esposito, White River Junction

A: If the varnish is in good shape (not cracking or flaking) just roughen the surface by going over it well with sandpaper. Paint first with an oil-base primer, and then put on your final coat. The important thing is that you use an oil-base paint. Latex won't adhere to the varnish.

KNOT HOLES SHOWING THROUGH PAINT

Q: Three months ago I painted my bathroom. I prepared the walls by scrubbing and lightly sanding them. I primed and used a latex paint. The room had previously been painted with an oil-base paint. Now knot holes are showing through. Is it because I used latex paint over oil paint? What can I do?

Rich, Windsor

A: The problem lies not with using latex over an oil base but with the kind of primer you used. Pine knots are notorious for bleeding through paint of all kinds. The solution is to use an alcohol-based primer and to cover the knot holes. We have had success with two brands, Bin and KILZ. You can use either to prime the entire surface or just the knot holes. Be sure to lightly sand before you prime. The alcohol-based primers are also fast drying and have a good adhesion quality for the finish paint.

HOMEMADE MILK-BASE PAINT

Q: I am rebuilding my barn and using fresh sawn lumber. I am wondering whether you can give the pros and cons of using a homemade milk-base paint. Do you have a formula for a subdued red, and can I use powdered or goat's milk? I would like to know where to purchase powder for coloring.

Jules, Fair Haven

A: We wish you had told us why you want to use a milk-base paint rather than the commercial latex or oil-base paints that are available on the market. If you were thinking of it in terms of economy, the yellow and red ochres (iron oxides, a by-product of iron mining) used to color the paints have become very expensive, and in the quantity you would need would be prohibitive. To give you some idea, a milk-base paint that is commercially available (manufactured by Trendlines in Chelsea, Massachusetts, and described by the company as "old-fashioned home-made milk paint") costs $11.50 a quart. If you were thinking in terms of durability, milk-based paints were rarely used on the outside of buildings. Unlike linseed-oil-based paints or stains, they did not penetrate the wood and so were not as durable.

Tom Visser of Vermont's Division for Historic Preservation gave us a typical "outbuilding" recipe for old-fashioned *oil-base* paint: 50 pounds yellow or red ochre, 100 pounds sifted road dust, mixed together with linseed oil. Then add soft soap until in a condition for spreading with a brush. Many farmers just mixed ochre with linseed oil and brushed it on straight. Incidentially, up around your neck of the woods, ochres (yellow and red) were both cheap and readily available in the 19th century, as Brandon was the center of a thriving iron-mining industry, which eventually became the Brandon Paint Works. The reason old-timers used milk (or blood, or organic glues or all three) in their paints was that when the water in them evaporated, the protein they contained coagulated and congealed, causing the paint to adhere to the surface. Tom said that the soft colors one sees on old barns today are not a result of the original pigments or ingredients used to mix the paints but rather of aging. The consensus among everyone we talked with was that you'd be better off buying regular paint for your barn rather than making it yourself.

REMOVING PAINT

Q: I have an older house, about 70 years old, that has had all the inside woodwork painted; window frames, baseboards, doors, etc. I would like to strip the paint off so it would be all natural wood again. I've used liquid stripper and sanded, but this is very messy. Is there a practical way of doing this without the mess? Every carpenter I've talked to says strippers or sanding are my only options.

Joan, Springfield

A: There are other ways of removing paint, we discovered. The first is a heat gun. It looks like a hair dryer and is reputed to be easy to use. Practice is important so you can judge how fast the gun works and can avoid scorching the wood. It's best to practice on some painted boards outside where, if there's a burst of flame, it will do no harm. It's a slow process, but there are no chemicals, and the mess is minimal. For a flat surface, use the gun in one hand and a putty knife with a scraping blade in the other. As soon as the paint starts to bubble, slide the scraper underneath it and lift the paint. Don't let the paint cool, as it will harden and stick to the wood. On moldings, corners, etc., use a toothbrush-sized wire brush, available at hardware or welding-supply stores. You probably will have to use one final application of chemical stripper, as heat guns can't remove all the paint. Another product we discovered is Peel-Away. It's expensive but apparently works well. First you paint on a liquid stripper and then you put a fiberglass resin cloth over the area. When the cloth is removed the paint is pulled off with it.

READER FEEDBACK: Betty Jaquay, a professional painter and paperhanger from Tinmouth, wrote, "In regard to stripping paint with a heat gun: *caution!* Old paint has lead in it, and heating it can release toxic fumes. Regardless of the method used, when stripping paint you should have adequate ventilation and wear a mask that protects against fumes and particles—the kind of mask that makes you look like Darth Vader. All substances removed by stripping should be treated as toxic waste and disposed of accordingly. Also, when using a heat gun, be careful about overheating areas behind spots being stripped, as fires have been started this way. Before undertaking the enormous task of stripping a whole house it is prudent to try a few test spots in unobtrusive corners. If woodwork was painted in the first place, there will be paint in the wood, and it will never look like natural wood again. If it was varnished first and then painted, however it may be worth the effort."

Sharon Nimtz, of Wallingford, wrote us about the vast experience she and her husband have acquired over the years stripping paint. Her nice, chatty letter concluded, "Nothing makes wood stripping easy, but in our rather large experience we've found paint scrapers the simplest."

PLASTER

Q: Do you know where we can purchase plaster such as professional plasterers use? We do not want just ordinary patching plaster which is used for patching small holes and cracks and looks like spackling compound. Our repair jobs are larger, such as repairing plaster that is falling from lath. Regular patching plaster doesn't seem to work on these jobs. We used to buy Rutland Patching Plaster, which was gray and worked well for us, but it's no longer available. We have asked local contractors and building-supply centers and all they seem to have is the white patching plaster.

Phil and Louise Dodge, Topsham

A: We found the plaster that you're loking for. It's called Structolite and comes in 50-pound bags. Many large building supply firms carry this product.

VINYL WALLPAPER

Q: I have a question about wallpaper that I can't find a consistent answer to. Can vinyl wallpaper be applied on a wall painted with a special vapor-barrier paint or over old vinyl paper? We have an old house without insulation and poor plaster walls with one layer of vinyl paper that's doing a great job holding the walls together. We want to insulate, and the vinyl paper makes a great vapor barrier. Since vapor barriers are made not to let any moisture through and vinyl papers do the same, will the paste dry? We feel we can save some time and money now if we can paper over the paper that's up, and in a few years, when our children are older and when we have more time, we can put up new walls. We're afraid of going ahead without your answer for fear of making more work and expense. We feel a lot of people must have the same question with more and more people insulating and painting a vapor barrier on their walls. It seems most wallpapers are vinyl or vinyl coated these days.

Michele Larson, Barre

A: We trotted down to Jim's Paints, in Windsor, and spoke to Jim about your question. He assured us that it's possible to put vinyl wallpaper over both vapor-barrier paints and old vinyl wallpaper. If the vinyl wallpaper that is going over old vinyl paper is fabric-backed (if it's fabric-backed it will have teeny threads on the back), you use a special paste. The brand he carries is called Shur-Stik, and it's described as a vinyl-to-vinyl adhesive. It sells for about $9 a gallon. If you are going to use a woven-backed vinyl wallpaper (smooth on the back), you use a special sizing such as a product called Wall-grip. It's also possible to paper over vapor-barrier paint by using Wall-grip.

CHAPTER 8

CATS AND DOGS

Until we started writing our column, we thought we were the only people in the world with pets who sporadically decided to become incontinent, whether out of vengeance, stupidity or biological needs beyond their control. The volume of letters we have received over the years asking for the ultimate solution for urine stains, smells and general damage has made us realize that we are not alone—nor are our animals. We have recommended a variety of remedies, none of which really and truly works. A couple of humid summer days is proof of the pudding. Our question is: "If we can put a man on the moon, how come we can't develop a product that will repair the damage to our rugs, floors and nose?" We no longer expect an answer, at least within our lifetimes.

"HOT SPOTS" AND FLEA BITES

Q: I can't believe it! We've had four hard frosts, my dog is wearing a new flea collar and is still getting "hot spots" which my vet tells me are an allergy to flea bites. Could there be something else wrong?

Sick and Tired, Woodstock

86

A: Probably not. First, no matter what kind of flea powder, collar or shampoo you use, the flea has to bite the dog in order to ingest the poison and die. As your dog's allergy (or nonspecific dermatitis) is caused by the flea's saliva, we are lead to the basic Catch-22 of flea allergies. Flea bites dog, flea dies—but it's too late because the dog has already begun to itch and develop a new skin-allergy spot. Second, before the flea dies it has probably managed to lay numerous eggs between the hairs of your pet. When the animal moves around or lies down, those eggs are dislodged and drop onto the floor or wherever your dog sleeps. Within three weeks, a whole new generation of fleas will have hatched.

Our vet says that research is now concentrating not on keeping fleas off the animal but rather removing them from the environment with minimal danger to humans. There are also pills available for dogs that discourage fleas: check with your vet.

Treat the hot spots as soon as they appear: cut the hair around them as short as possible and apply a few drops of a product called Tresaderm, which is available from your vet. It works amazing healing wonders. If the hot spots have become seriously weepy, your vet will probably give your dog a shot of cortisone.

ANIMAL ACCOMMODATIONS

Q: I need to know where I can find a list of motels that allow dogs for the night, as we plan to take our dog with us when we drive down to Florida this fall.

G. M. H., Windsor

A: *Fodor's USA* carries the information you need. If you are a member, AAA also has a directory that lists motels, hotels and inns where pets are welcome.

DOG-BREEDER RESOURCES

Q: I am looking for a breeder of toy fox terriers in the state or nearby. The terriers must have black-and-white markings.

C. Martin, Worcester

A: Write to the American Kennel Club, 51 Madison Ave., New York, NY 10010, enclosing a stamped, self-addressed envelope. They'll provide you with the name of the president of the Toy Fox Terrier Breeder Association. You can get in touch with that person and discuss your puppy needs. Alternatively, if you are near a store that stocks a wide variety of magazines, buy a copy of *Dog World* (or see if your library can get a copy for you) and look in the Classifieds for toy fox terrier breeders.

THE WANDERING DOG

Q: I live in the country, but I have had bad luck with my mixed-breed dogs because they have a tendency to wander. My last pet was hit by a car. I have heard that English shepherds are a good, stay-at-home breed, but they are not AKC registered, and I don't know where to find one. Can you help?

Sherry Olsen, Plainfield

A: Before you get a puppy, thoroughbred or mixed breed, we suggest you read a book called *How to Be Your Dog's Best Friend* by the Monks of New Skete, published by Little, Brown and Co. These monks not only train dogs but owners as well. Their contention is that when a dog has a problem it is because the owner has either allowed or inadvertently caused the problem to happen. In their book the monks devote a lot of space to the subject of "the wandering dog." Dogs, like their ancestor the wolf, are social animals. To the monks' way of thinking, the wandering habit has nothing to do with the breed but rather the manner in which and the extent to which the dog has been socialized into the family and has come to accept the family as its "pack." Too often, the monks note, country dog owners have the idea that their dog should be left outside all day (and sometimes all night) because it is happier that way. What actually happens is the dog, feeling lonely and excluded from its human pack, ranges over an ever-widening territory in search of companionship. Eventually it either finds the companionship it is seeking or meets with an accident—or, as is increasingly the case, particularly in rural areas, a dognapper. The latter sell the unfortunate animals to hospitals and research centers.

NONALLERGENIC CATS

Q: I have heard several times that Siamese cats are nonallergenic. Are they? I also need to know if that would apply not only to persons with a cat allergy but to those with asthma as well. If Siamese are not nonallergenic is there an injection for a cat or a person that will help? If so, how much would it cost? I need to know as soon as possible. A member of my family has the conditions listed above. My mother wants a cat. Siamese are her favorite.

Reader in Rutland Town

A: There is no breed of cat that is nonallergenic. The reason is that, unlike some breeds of dogs, all cats shed. They also give off something called "cat dander," which is a very fine, highly allergenic dandruff. There are, of course, shots that people can take for allergies, but they are costly and must be administered fairly frequently. Asthma is another complicating factor, but asthmatic reactions are so different from person to person that it would be impossible to make any generalizations concerning them. There is no shot that will make a cat nonallergenic. If someone invented one, he would be a millionaire overnight. Has your mother ever considered the beauties of tropical fish?

ODORS, STAINS AND OTHER UNPLEASANTNESS

Q: Do you know some magic that will remove the odor of dog urine from an oriental carpet? I have tried water, various household cleaners, carpet-cleaning powders and sprinkling cat litter under and on top of the stained area for several days. Any other ideas? And while we're at it, is there anything that really gets out the smell of skunk?

M., Shelburne

A: About a year ago one of Anne's dogs had an encounter with a skunk, and Anne tried all the home remedies, from tomato juice to cider vinegar. Although either singly or in combination they removed the worst of the odor (the high acid content of the above agents cuts through the oil in which the skunk scent is suspended), a stubborn aura of skunkiness remained, particularly when the weather turned humid. Then one day, browsing around in a feed store, Anne happened upon a product called Skunk Kleen and decided to try it. Miracle of miracles, it worked! Anne was so thrilled that she called Mr. G. G. Bean of Brunswick, Maine, whose name was on the bottle as manufacturer. She was curious as to the ingredients of this wonderful stuff. Mr. Bean wouldn't tell. "It's a secret," he said, "but it's completely safe and natural. It took me five years to develop, and I don't want anybody to steal my idea." Mr. Bean told us about a number of other products he had invented, among them something called Urine Kleen. "It doesn't mask with perfumes," he said. "It takes away the smell by neutralizing it, which other products don't do." He very kindly sent us a bottle, we tried it on an oriental rug that we think was probably in worse shape than M.'s, and it performed just as Mr. Bean said it would. If you can't find Mr. Bean's products in your area (look around in pet stores and farm-supply places) write him at G.G. Bean, Inc., P.O. Box 638, Brunswick, ME 04011.

Q: Several weeks ago you published the name and address of a man in Maine who manufactures spot remover especially for removing dog urine from rugs. Can you reprint it?

Pauline, Barre

A: Mr. Bean's product does not remove spots, only odors. The best thing for preventing spots on rugs is to pour a liberal quantity of white vinegar and water, mixed in equal amounts, on the offending (still wet) area and sponge up with a paper towel. Follow this with an equally liberal application of soda water. Sponge up. This will work on cat urine as well, but not on cat spray. For that, use Mr. Bean's Skunk Kleen. Skunk and cat spray are basically the same thing: a scent marker suspended in body-oil secretions. Spotting may occur in spite of your efforts. Urine contains a high percentage of ammonia, which acts as a bleach on certain dyes. The ammonia, in combination with the uric acid that is also found in urine, may change the color of your carpet.

Q: How do you get animal urine stains out of wood floors?
Bill, Waterbury

A: We didn't know the answer, but Frank Palumbo, of Warren, who is a professional floor refinisher, did. He wrote, "First, sand away the old finish with 60-grit sandpaper, then bleach out with a solution of oxalic acid crystals (available from your pharmacist). Dissolve the crystals in warm water to the point of saturation. Let stand overnight in a glass jar. Warm mixture and apply on stains with a brush. Let dry. Remove residue that remains with a solution of 50-percent water and 50-percent white vinegar. Lightly hand sand area with 100-grit sandpaper and reapply whatever finish is on the floor."

Q: What does one use to keep a cat from sitting in a windowbox? I've tried pet-spray repellent (Boundry), and it didn't help at all. Also, what (besides my shotgun) will keep my dog out of the garden?
Nancy Bambera, Dorset

A: Mrs. Muriel Link, of Springfield, might have the answer (we've never tried it, so aren't positive): "Mothballs didn't keep cats away, but creosote did. Cats were writing their identification on my porch until I painted sections with creosote, the same color as my house. I might suggest dipping strips of cloth in creosote and hanging them where you are bothered."

As to keeping your dogs out of the garden, we have no solution other than a fence (or an intensive aversion training program).

CAT-BOX LITTER

Q: For several years my mother has been putting used litter from my cat around her flowers and on the grass. Now a chemical deodorant has been added to litter, and I wonder if this is harmful to the soil?

Lois Wheeler, Windsor

A: We had always believed that putting used cat litter, deodorized or not, on any living or growing thing would instantly cause wilting, yellowing and certain death. We were therefore more than a little nonplussed by your question. We put a call in to the folks who manufacture Kleen Kitty and talked to one of their research chemists. He told us that it is perfectly fine to put used cat litter on your lawn, flower bed or compost, and that the materials used in the deodorant are ecologically perfectly safe. He did give us a word of caution, however. Cat excrement sometimes contains a virus that causes toxoplasmosis. Should a pregnant woman become infected, there will be serious damage to the fetus, so the chemist recommended that litter not be used on vegetable gardens. He also told us that cat litter is made from a type of clay that, if mixed with vegetable oil and stored in a closed container, is likely to spontaneously combust. We pass this information on, not because we think it will change any lives but because it is an interesting bit of trivia.

DE-CLAWING CATS: PROS AND CONS (ALL EMOTIONAL)

Q: We are wondering if somebody out there can help us find a way to stop our much-loved cat from scratching on the sides of a couch and on wallpaper. We bought a scratching post: No go. She won't use it. We clip her nails frequently, but she seems to prefer to scratch the walls and the couch. Any ideas, short of casting her out into the cold, cruel world, would be appreciated.

Trish Feld, Waterbury

A: Our source at the Windsor Animal Clinic suggests a squirt of very cold water in the cat's face, when Mr. Cat is engaged in scratching wallpaper and couch. As *consistent* aversive training, that should do the trick. The problem is that if the cat is left alone for long periods of time during the day, the occasional blast of water won't teach its lesson. He said that once cats acquire bad habits, there is little one can do except have them de-clawed.

READER FEEDBACK: Letter upon letter flooded in, all filled with outrage! Megan Martel, of Waterbury, wrote: "You told Trish Feld to de-claw her cat. That means breaking every first bone of the toe of the claw. This is not good for the cat because it has to protect itself. Also it is very painful." Suzanne Montalvan, of Orwell, sent in a quote from *Dr. Pitcairn's Complete Guide to Natural Health For Dogs and Cats*: "The practice of removing their claws (which is equivalent to cutting off the last joint of each of your fingers) is not only cruel and painful but prevents the important feline exercise of kneading and stretching which benefits the muscles of the forelegs, backbone and shoulders." Amazed by this outpouring, we conducted a further investigation. Polling a number of city vets who treat cats exclusively (there are no specialized cat vets around here, at least so far), we discovered that cat veterinarians think de-clawing is acceptable if the cat is never allowed outside and if the procedure is done before the animal is four months old.

CHAPTER 9

HOUSE INVADERS

We have a pretty laid-back attitude toward "house invaders." We're grateful that these foragers of air and field content themselves with being nuisances, helping themselves to no more than they need in contrast to their human (and mostly urban) counterparts. We also know that if a house-invader problem is urgent we (and all our readers) have recourse to county or district Extension Services, which exist in every state in the US and are there to answer questions and offer solutions to almost every practical problem a householder, gardener or farmer may face in the course of a day, a season or a year.

CLUSTER FLIES

Q: Ugh! Yuck! It's that time of year again when our 130-year-old house is overrun with big, slow, black, fuzzy flies. Throughout the winter new ones appear every day. They are especially disgusting when we rewarm the house after a weekend away. The only good thing about them is that they are so slow they can be sucked up with a vacuum cleaner. Is there any safe way to control these replusive creatures, or can you at least find any information that will soften my attitude to them?

M. T., Plainfield

A: The revolting creatures in question are called cluster flies. They belong to the same family as flesh flies and blowflies and are a distant relation of the housefly. Their larvae (maggots) are parasitic on earthworms, particularly the variety found in cattle manure. Chances are there are cattle or horses pastured somewhere near your house. Cluster flies are not really harmful: they do not breed inside buildings, they are not attracted to foods in the home and they do not present any recognized health hazard. During the summer, cluster flies feed on nectar and fruit juices; as soon as cold weather comes they look for warm places, like your house, in which to hibernate. They enter buildings by squeezing through any tiny crack they can find and take up residence in the partitions. Wakened by the heat of a room warmed to more than 54 degrees they will emerge and start flying around, thinking it's spring. They'll probably persist until spring actually does arrive. On the first warm day open all your windows, and they will go away for the summer months.

ANTS

Q: I read that the best way to get rid of carpenter ants is Terro Ant Killer. The ants carry it back to their nests and kill the whole colony. Can you tell me where to get it?

J. M., Rutland

A: Although the Vermont Department of Agriculture has licensed Terro Ant Killer for sale, they caution that it is such a hideous poison that under no circumstances should it be used in houses where there are children and/or pets. Its main ingredient is sodium arsenate, which will last in residue form in your house forever. Anne once had a plague of carpenter ants that was cured by a Christian Scientist practitioner who came to her house and quite literally prayed them away. They have never come back. As an alternative you might call your Extension Service agent and ask him for his advice, giving him the details of the extent and area of your carpenter ant infestation. There are many compounds which when properly used are just as effective as Terro, and far safer.

Q: The other day I heard of a mixture that is supposed to get rid of ants. It is 2 tablespoons of detergent and 2 tablespoons of Epsom salts in 1 gallon of water. This does not sound strong enough to me. Can you advise?

B. J. B., Rutland

A: There are as many home remedies for getting rid of ants as there are kinds of ants in homes. Each kind is attracted to different foods and conditions. Some like damp, some like dry, some like sweets, others like crumbs and still others like grease. Some ants just like to hang around the house and be a nuisance. The consensus seems to be that the first, essential step is to find where they are coming into the house. Then remedies differ. A number of our readers swear that sprinkling black or cayenne pepper around the ant interstate (or, if you can afford it, around the whole house foundation) works wonders. Others suggest drawing a chalk line around where they are coming in, and still others say white flour is just as effective.

There certainly isn't any harm in trying your Epsom salts mixture and, if it doesn't seem effective, either decrease the amount of water or increase the amount of detergent and salts. If it still doesn't get rid of the ants, then it probably doesn't work.

BEETLES

Q: How damaging is the worm that leaves a tiny pinhole from which drops a light-yellow dust from below my pine timbers? The timbers sound solid when hit with a hammer.

C. McN., Rutland

A: It sounds to us as though your timbers have a case of powder-post beetles, and they can destroy a structure. There are many varieties, but the most common is the old-house borer. These creatures tunnel in wood of all sorts, and their larvae feed on the cellulose starch in the wood. The Extension Service of Vermont has a great information sheet (Bulletin EL 51) on different kinds of beetles and how to control them. Another that is helpful is

APC No. 829, "Household/Structural Pest Control." If the infestation (and piles of sawdust) increase, call an exterminator. Nan's husband worked on a US government restoration project in which one of the buildings was loaded with powder-post beetles. The feds brought an exterminator to New England from Florida. The building was tented and gassed for two days. The beetles died, but the cost was over $25,000, and the beetles were back in two years.

CRICKETS

Q: We have lived in our house for many years and have never had this problem. We are bothered by a loud chirping, and although we can't see them, we suspect that they are crickets. They have chirped night and day for two months. Our house is insulated. Have you any solution? Would sonar waves help?

Annoyed, Springfield

A: It sounds like crickets to us. They come into the house when it begins to turn cold outside; they could have gained access through the cellar, on wood you brought in, or just through the door. We suggest you follow the chirping to its source. Crickets like dark, warm places: around hearths, under cabinets in the bathroom or clothes closets are good places to start. When you catch them (they aren't difficult to catch) you can dispose of them as you will. The Chinese keep them around the house in cages, for good luck. Since you haven't seen even one cricket, we doubt you have anything near an infestation. Three or four crickets can make enough racket to sound like 100. But do try to get rid of them, as they feed voraciously on wool and cotton and have a particular fondness for rugs and carpets.

READER FEEDBACK: Ferris Harris, of Proctorsville, wrote: "The question of chirping noises brought to mind the experience of a family member. She also heard chirping and found the source was a smoke detector in a drawer. It had been there some time, and when the battery got weak, it chirped, as described in Annoyed's letter."

ANNOYED REPLIED: "Thank you so much for your help in solving our cricket problem. We put a new battery in our smoke detector and it did the job! No more chirping!"

Moths

Q: Is there anything better than mothballs, gas or flakes to control moths in closets and dresser drawers? Something that does not leave a strong odor?

Ruthie, Castleton

A: We suggest you get some cedar chips from your farm-supply store or lumberyard. Or just buy them in the pet section of your supermarket. Fill some old nylon stockings with chips, and hang them in your closet. For moth control in bureau drawers: moths— or to be more exact, their larvae—for some reason won't devour things that are newly washed or dry-cleaned and, as much as we hate to admit it (given our means of livelihood) they are repelled by newspaper. So make sure the garments you are going to store are clean, then layer them with newspaper. You might also want to make small packets of cedar chips to put between the layers as an added precaution.

Fleas

Q: We are searching desperately for a nonchemical and non-ultrasonic solution to fleas in our home. We took an apartment over three months ago, little knowing that the wall-to-wall carpeting was infested with fleas! Being pregnant and with a young child, I am loath to resort to chemicals and wonder if you or any of your readers have discovered a natural, effective way to get rid of fleas. We have no pets, but the critters don't seem to mind feeding on *us!* An exterminator told us we would have fleas for three months or so if we didn't spray, but the time is up and no sign of abatement. Any tips or encouraging words?

Bugged, Montpelier

A: We couldn't discover any alternatives to poisons or sprays until we got this letter from Elizabeth Willbanks, of Wells: "In the room that has the most fleas, or in each room, put a dish filled with water and a light over the dish so that it is shining on the water. Put several drops of dish detergent in the water and turn on the light at night (I use the clip-on kind). Make sure no other lights are on.

The fleas will be attracted to the light and fall into the water and drown. The dish soap breaks the surface tension of the water so that the fleas fall in rather than bounce off. Keep the light on until there are no more fleas caught, and then keep it on after that to catch the batches of fleas that will hatch from new eggs. I had the same problem when I lived in Florida. I had the house professionally fumigated twice and still had fleas. I tried the above (I read it in *Mother Earth News*), and it finally got rid of them for good."

RODENTS: MICE, RATS, AND SQUIRRELS

Q: I am overrun with field mice. I was never bothered until this past winter, and they are still coming in. I've caught 10 in three days. I have 6 mouse traps set. I don't dare have a cat, as I have a parrot. I've always used d-Con, but it doesn't seem to have any effect on these little creatures.

Lil, West Rutland

A: Determine where the mice are nesting in your house. They rarely travel in more than a 10- to 20-foot radius from their nest as long as there is an adequate supply of food and water. It is therefore highly unlikely that they are going back and forth between outdoors and indoors.

Droppings, gnawings, holes, tracks in the dust (if you are one of those people who have no dust, sprinkle some flour around the mice's approximate location) and noise will help you find the nests. Place the traps and d-Con as close to them as you can. The active ingredient in d-Con is Warfarin, a slow-acting decoagulant which takes from three to five days to work. If there are tastier things around to eat, the mice may ignore it, and an addition of sugar or vegetable oil will make the poison more attractive. (Don't use sugar during warm weather, though, as it will cause the d-Con to mold and, understandably, the mice won't touch it.) Mice have 5 to 10 young per litter and from 6 to 10 litters a year. They mature in 2 to 3 months, so it's no wonder the problem escalates so quickly!

Once you locate what we assume has now reached the proportions of a colony, seal up any cracks in the area where mice can get either in or out. Remember, mice can squeeze through really tiny spaces. Keep using the d-Con along with the traps. You should be rid of the mice in three or four weeks.

Q: Please help us with a perennial rat problem. We live in an old farmhouse that has more holes that you can possibly patch. Each year the rats outsmart the barn cats or scare them off, then they rattle around the kitchen. We finally resorted to d-Con Bait-bits— an exclusive blend of natural ingredients—and the house stinks of rotting rat. How can we get rid of this stench besides perfume spray or dismantling the walls? And what do we do to get rid of the rats altogether?

Verandah Porche, Guilford

A: Ever consider moving? Aside from that, the only thing that will get rid of the stench in the walls is time, which isn't much help if the rats keep dying in them. As to getting rid of the rats altogether, the first order of business is to destroy their nesting habitat, which, if you have a barn, is virtually impossible. You can, however, start a baiting program in the barn as well as keeping one up in the house. It helps, by the way, if you store all the barn feed in closed metal containers. After you start the baiting program, keep it up long after you think you've got the problem under control, and also keep the bait fresh. As our Extension Service agent remarked, "You wouldn't want to eat four-day-old meatloaf, would you?" Also, when you are setting the bait out, cover your hands with plastic bags: otherwise the rats will smell human on the bait and stay away. In your kitchen keep all food in glass or metal containers or in the icebox or an insulated chest. The rats won't come in if there isn't anything for them to eat. If you have a cellar they may be living down there. Clean out any old rags, newspapers, etc., in which they might be nesting, and do your best to seal up any holes in the foundation. And finally, how about bringing a couple of barn cats into the house at night?

Q: Problem: red squirrels residing within the house. The d-Con disappears, but the running around overhead continues. The feedstore tells me that d-Con is ineffective on squirrels, as all they do is "squirrel" it away. What will kill them, now that effective poisons are off the market?

Ted Edmunds, Poultney

A: Let us first consider the alternatives to extermination. The chances are you have nut- and/or cone-bearing trees close to your house, and the squirrels are using your attic as a conveniently located storage area. Obviously you do not wish to cut down your trees in order to get rid of the squirrels, but you can closely examine the outside of your house to see where they are coming in. Despite the racket they make, squirrels are small animals and can squeeze through cracks and crevices as small as 1 ½ inches. Seal the holes tighly with tin flashing or flattened tin cans, securely nailed around the edges. This method ensures two things: first, that you will no longer be bothered by existing squirrels, and second, that you won't be bothered by a new generation next year. If you don't care about next year you can bait them with a Havahart trap and release them at least two miles from your house. Or you can call an exterminator.

Q: I have a problem—not bats in the belfry, but squirrels in the attic. I've tried ways to drive them out with no success. A contraption referred to as an "ultrasonic sound device" has been mentioned to me. It's supposed to get rid of rats, mice and squirrels in your house. If you have any information about a device of this sort, I will be grateful to learn about it.

Elizabeth Lamphere, Calais

A: These ultrasonic devices were all the rage a couple of years ago, but proved to be just about 100-percent ineffective. The USDA, as well as consumer groups, conducted extensive tests on the devices and could find no scientific or practical evidence to substantiate the claims made for them by their manufacturers. The old ways are best. Seal the cracks and crawl holes between the eaves, window frames and walls of your attic, and if, after that, you still want to try an ultrasonic device, we'll bet you anything you'll be able to pick one up at someone's yard sale come spring. Cheap.

BATS

Q: We have an old house with an unfinished attic and find we have bats. What can we use to get rid of them? We have tried all sorts of sprays and d-Con, but nothing has helped.

S. J. R., Rutland

A: First off, forget the sprays. Bats are mammals. Insecticides, etc., may make them sick but won't kill them. Second, forget the d-Con. Bats feed primarily on flying insects and are completely uninterested in grain or seed. What you need to do is shoo the bats out of your attic. Use bright lights and moth repellent: from the time the first bat leaves, it will take about 20 minutes for the entire colony to disperse. Then you must bat-proof. Check to see where the bats are coming in and going out, close all openings greater than 3/8-inch wide. Renail boards and flashing, use mesh hardware cloth and pack cracks with steel wool or other packing material, cover with caulking compound and paint. Be sure and check places where electrical wires enter the house. Then keep an eye on the outside of the house, and if the bats are still coming to call, repeat the light/mothball process and look for more openings. Good luck!

CHAPTER 10

OUTDOOR PESTS

It always seems that something is going to get in the way of perfection. You work your fingers to the bone and the yard and garden look like a photograph in an expensive, glossy magazine. Your pride is palpable. Bang! You wake up in the morning and some creature, or combination of them, has either ruined everything or is in the process of doing so. Or you try to be kind and feed the birds when suddenly every awful bird imaginable is at your feeder and the pretty, well-mannered birds you would prefer are nowhere in sight. There are solutions to some imperfections in life. To other imperfections, there are none. Read on.

SPIDERS

Q: How do you get rid of spiders permanently? The outside of my house, the porch, the eaves and the garage are just loaded with huge, fat ones. We tried spraying. It kills them off for a while, but new ones appear. Any advice would be helpful.

S. F., Plainfield

A: If the spray you are using is a bug insecticide, you are killing the spiders' dinner rather than the spiders. The reason the spiders disappear for a while is that after you spray there isn't anything for them to eat. As spiders are arachnids and belong to the same family as plant mites and aphids, what you need is an insecticide plant spray. You might also consider turning out your outside lights or replacing the bulbs with yellow "bug lights." Generally it is outside lights which attract the bugs which attract the spiders in the first place.

There are, in the opinion of experts, no poisonous spiders in Vermont and though they might not be the loveliest looking creatures in the world, spiders are actually very beneficial. We were brought up to believe they are good luck (probably because they helped control the fly population in our cow barn), and due to that early training we even go so far as to gently remove the spiders that have gotten into our house and put them back outdoors.

BLACK FLIES

Q: It's nearly black fly time, and my husband loves to go fishing and likes me to come along. But I have a hideous allergy to the horrible little creatures. I've tried virtually every bug repellent on the market, and nothing works. Any suggestions?

No Welts Please, Brandon

A: The mother of a young Marine, stationed at Parris Island, told us (with some amusement) that the fellows down there have been using Avon's Skin-So-Soft for years. Although intended as a bath oil, it is apparently also the ultimate bug dope. We took a bottle of it to our dermatologist, who said there was nothing in it that would cause irritation if used directly on the skin. Subsequently we read in the *Wall Street Journal* that a horse trainer in Maryland uses the product on his horses to keep the flies at bay!

CHINCH BUGS

Q: Is there an inexpensive treatment for lawns being ruined by chinch bugs?

Concerned Springfielders

A: As soon as the initial damage is noted in June, treat your lawn with a registered lawn insecticide or any granular or powdered insecticide containing carbaryl. Irrigate the lawn before treatment with 1 to 1 ½ inches of water or wait for a heavy rain; then follow the instructions on the label. A second application may be necessary two or three weeks later as well as a third in mid-August.

MOLES

Q: I'm having trouble with moles in the lawn. Every recommendation by the hardware store is to no avail. Any suggestions?
Bancroft Dwinnell, Montpelier

A: There isn't much you can do about them once spring has come, although you can frighten them away from current burrowings by the simple expedient of going to your local toy store and purchasing some pinwheels. Place them, stick down, in the ground. The vibration of the breeze-turned wheels will frighten the moles off, at least from a small area.

To keep the moles from coming back the following spring, all you have to do is remove their food supply, which consists of insect grubs and eggs. (They are particularly fond of rose chafer and Japanese beetle grubs.) In early July, when the pests are laying their eggs in your lawn, sprinkle the ground with Diazinon crystals, available at your local hardware, garden or feed store. Some lawn fertilizers, such as Scott's, incorporate pesticides; check the label on the bag.

Incidentally, contrary to popular myth, moles do not, because they cannot, eat bulbs and tubers. Their mouths and teeth are too tiny. The culprits are meadow mice, who use the tunnels the moles have dug.

E. Abbott, of Barre, sent us a hint for the mole/meadow mouse problem: "I mixed one tablespoon of ammonia (not the sudsy kind) in one quart of water and watered my sprouting plants about three inches from the stems, at least two or three times a week for two or three weeks. Then once every two weeks. This will discourage moles and mice and give a brighter color to the leaves and flowers. The treatment is good for house plants too."

WOODCHUCKS

Q: I own a driving range. The woodchucks are co-owners. They dig holes large enough to make my golf balls disappear. How can I get rid of them?

Ilse Vergi, North Clarendon

A: We read this letter to our County agent who said, "Has she ever tried exploding golf balls?" He then went on, in a more serious vein, to say that the best time to get rid of these pesky critters is in late July or early August. Then you can either trap them in a Havahart trap (available on loan, at no cost, from your game warden) or kill them. Either way you will have to find their exit, or escape hole (the one without the dirt mound) and block it up. To trap woodchucks, the best method is to fill a five-gallon drum with water, pour it down the hole and flood them out. To kill them, gas pellets are available at most hardware and feed stores.

By the way, we both have dogs and have always assumed that is why neither of us have ever had a woodchuck problem.

READER FEEDBACK: Ms. Vergi's question prompted an outpouring of suggestions from our readers, each one more vicious than the last. They ranged from fitting a hose to the exhaust pipe of your car, putting the hose down the hole and idling the engine for a while to (literally) blowing up the burrow with gunpowder to this, from Robert Morse, of Williamstown: "Take an old rag about 14- to 24-inches square, or the leg of a pair of pants. Use about that much cloth. Then take some gasoline from the can you fill your lawnmower with and soak the rag with gasoline. Put the rag in the woodchuck hole, cover the hole over with a rock or a board and put some dirt around the edges so no raw gas fumes will come out. I have yet to see a woodchuck come out after this treatment. Be sure you are not smoking when you do this."

SQUIRRELS AND BIRDS

Q: I have a small vegetable garden. Last year the birds and squirrels dug up the seeds as soon as they were planted. In fact they got all the pea and corn seeds. Any suggestions?

A. F. D., Rutland

A: There is a product called Crow-Chex that is sold at feed-and-grain stores. You dip your seeds in it before planting; it's foul tasting to both birds and squirrels.

Q: Help! Short of using gunfire, there must be a way! My husband put a bird-feeding station in our side yard, and I've four feeders that I fill with a mixture of sunflower seeds and cracked corn. We have a variety of breakfast, lunch and dinner guests at the feeding station, all very polite and delighted with their meals. They even share with our two squirrels. But the pigeons! They have become a real problem. How on earth do I force them to move to downtown Rutland? Is there something I should (or should not) do? Something I can feed or not feed? If I leave the feeder empty during the summer, will the pigeons go away never to return? P.S. It should also be noted that the "house-warming" gifts the pigeons bring and leave for us as they perch on our roof are really not appreciated either.

Linda Matteson, Rutland

A: The best way to discourage pigeons is to replace your platform feeders with tube feeders; the perches will be too small for the substantial birds to perch on as they peck away. Tube feeders will also eliminate bluejays, mourning doves (which, despite their name, are actually a close relative of the pigeon) and some varieties of sparrow. All these, like pigeons, tend to be ground feeders and cracked corn is their food of choice. They can't get at the corn in a tube feeder. You can also try keeping the ground around the feeders clear of seed and corn, but that is, we know from experience, virtually impossible.

Other than the above, the only thing we can suggest is that every time you have a visitation of pigeons you leap out of the house, waving your arms and shouting, "Boo! Ha! Boo!" The drawbacks to this method are obvious.

By the way, please do *not* leave your feeders empty during the summer months. If you decide to feed the birds, you must make a commitment to do so all year round. Birds become dependent on the feeder as a source of food during the cold months. Suddenly taking that source away is a hardship tantamount to your being completely deprived of grocery money just because you have vegetables ripening in your garden.

SKUNKS

Q: If you can help us get rid of a skunk problem, we will be eternally grateful. So will our neighbors. As soon as there is a hint of spring, a skunk walks around our house, evidently getting as near to the cellar walls as possible and spraying merrily as he or she makes a circuit of the house. The smell is really overpowering. From reports the skunk does the same thing to most of the houses on our street. We've never seen the animal, but we are sure of its itinerary. We do not live in the country; ours is the usual city street.

Rachel B. Grenier, Barre

A: Skunks begin to breed in late February or early March, and your skunk is probably a male, marking out its territory and living happily out of neighborhood garbage cans. Having left its winter den, it has taken up its summer residence under a porch, in the foundation of an outbuilding or garage, or in someone's cellar.

The best method of control is for you (and your neighbors) to seal up any and all spaces through which the skunk might enter your house. Use boards or heavy wire mesh. As skunks are generally nocturnal animals, it is best to do this at night when they've left to go on foraging and/or mating expeditions. You can also drive them away by using moth flakes in their burrows, but you have to find their burrows first. Your local game warden will help you do this, and may even offer to trap the animal when found. You can find his number by looking under "Vermont-State of, Natural Resources Agency, Fish & Wildlife Dept." in your phone book.

To get rid of the smell the skunk has left behind during his circuit of your house, a mild solution of chlorine bleach and water poured over and around the offending area is usually effective.

By the time this letter is published, your skunk will most likely have stopped its malodorous nocturnal activities. Mating season is over by the middle of March. Unfortunately in late May and early June, the result of all this carrying on will appear in the form of litters of 2 to 16 kittens, so it's best to deal with the problem now, despite the fact that to all olfactory appearances it seems to have gone away.

SLUGS

Q: Our garden is close to a river, and because of this, the area is often quite damp. We have a terrible problem with slugs eating our vegetation. After a rainfall, there are literally hundreds of slugs in our garden! Do you know of any deterrent, preferably natural, that will keep these pests away from our vegetables?

B. B. W., East Poultney

A: We once read that a way to do slugs in was to place shallow containers filled with beer around the garden. It didn't work, at least not for us. We have had some success protecting tender plants by putting a thin line of wood ash along the row; the slugs' soft, moist bodies are sensitive to dry materials. Since your slug infestation is so great, however, we suggest you put cabbage leaves or pieces of plastic around your garden. The night-feeding slugs will gather together beneath these shelters during the day, and in the morning you can collect a pile of them and kill them.

READER FEEDBACK: R.L.D., of Waterbury Center, wrote that she uses a light sprinkling of salt to get rid of slugs. "They will curl up, turn brown and die in seconds. Try it. I would not advise sprinkling the entire garden with the salt shaker, but a little on the affected plants and around the base should do no harm." Mrs. H. Connor, of Woodstock, wrote that "anything scratchy or powdery helps: wood ash, coarse sand, limestone. But the best deterrent is diatomaceous earth: you can get it from places that carry swimming-pool supplies."

CHAPTER 11

GROWING FOOD AND FLOWERS

We've recently been reading (with some amusement) that gardening has become a fad among city-bred yuppies and their ilk. Vermonters are natural-born gardeners. One rarely passes a house that doesn't boast at least one flourishing garden, either vegetable or flower or a combination of the two. Traditionally, Town Meeting Day is the day to start seeds indoors for planting out on Memorial Day (or a little before or after). These are times of celebration for those of us who have been starved for the feel of earth and the sight of greenery during the long winter months. Gardens for us are a necessity, not only for the food they produce but the pleasure they provide. There are, of course, a few nettles in Paradise, such as weeds, blight, bugs and predators. But they go with the territory and, with a little work, care and forethought, can usually be dealt with.

ASPARAGUS AND SALT

Q: Asparagus, having had its origin along the shores of the Mediterranean Sea, should naturally thrive in a somewhat salty environment. From time to time I have heard from people about their father or grandfather's using rock salt or pork-salt brine on asparagus beds to keep down the grass and weeds. I had hesitated experimenting with salt on my established bed until I have still better information as to salt's safety before using this old-fashioned method.

Francis Clark, Morrisville

A: In the course of researching your question we discovered that asparagus that has "escaped" cultivation will often be found growing wild at the edge of salt marshes. In the south of England it flourishes along the perimeters of sandy beaches, which leads us to agree with your assumption that asparagus is salt-resistant. To make doubly sure, we called our friend David Talbot, who is not only a molecular biologist but also owner and proprietor of Talbot's Herb and Perennial Farm in Hartland. He said he could see no reason why rock salt or brine would damage your asparagus bed, although some weeds may turn out to be as resistant to salt as asparagus.

An alternative method of weed control is to scratch rye grass seed ("green manure") into your bed as soon as the last of the asparagus has been harvested. It will grow quickly and become a living mulch, choking out the weeds. By next spring it will have decomposed to a point where it is easy to pull out of the bed.

READER FEEDBACK: Donald Conger, of Brookfield, wrote: "About salt being put on asparagus: it is very, very safe and is very good for asparagus. I have used it on my asparagus beds for 30 years or more. Salt must be pure rock salt. Cover the ground well. It should be spread on in early spring."

BAMBOO

Q: We are having a problem with bamboo on our lot. How can we kill it? We cut it down, and it grows right back. Please help.

Myrt and Gert, Williamstown

A: Cutting down your bamboo isn't going to do a bit of good. Bamboo is not only extremely prolific but has a highly developed and extensive root system. We are not permitted by the State of Vermont to dispense information on most fungicides, herbicides, pesticides or insecticides (you must be licensed to do so), but as your County Agricultural Extension Agent is licensed in all categories, he'll be able to give you advice either over the phone or through a pamphlet called "New England Guide to Chemical Control of Problem Weeds and Brush" (1985). Specify that you want the guide that deals with the nine problem weeds in New England (bamboo, goldenrod, poison ivy, poison oak, blackberries, raspberries, and honeysuckle, among others). There are also single leaflets dealing with methods of controlling the above. These pamphlets and leaflets are free. In Vermont, your local Extension Service is listed under E in the White Pages of the telephone directory.

We did find out that there is a new chemical on the market that, when sprayed on bamboo leaves, is absorbed into the root system and kills the plants dead. This product is listed in the above Extension Service pamphlet.

ANIMALS

Q: Do you have any suggestions as to how to keep deer from nibbling the new shoots and tender bark on my fruit trees? I've done everything from spreading blood meal around the roots to, if you'll pardon the expression, urinating on the tree trunks. Nothing seems to work. Any suggestions?

F. A. B., Hartland

A: Take a trip down to your nearest barber or hairdresser and ask them to give you a bagful of hair clippings. Make up some mesh bags or cut the legs off your (or your wife's) stockings and make up some bags from them. Stuff with hair and hang from the branches of your trees. Human hair will preserve its scent far longer than blood meal or urine and will keep not only deer but other nibblers and gnawers at bay.

INSECTS

Q: Japanese beetles: what can you tell me about their control? The neighborhood seems overrun with them. They eat my flowers.

Maria Belanger, Montpelier

A: If the beetles are all over the neighborhood, it's hard for you to get rid of them without your neighbors joining in the effort. Anyway, this fall buy some milky-spore powder at your hardware store: that should get rid of the larve that are in *your* lawn, at least. In the spring buy a couple of Japanese beetle traps (also available at your hardware store) and ask your neighbors to do the same. As an inexpensive alternative, fill a coffee can with kerosene and manually brush the beetles off your flowers into the can: a few may fly away, but you'll get most of them.

Q: I have been told that a detergent-and-water solution is an effective insect deterrent when sprayed on shrubs, roses, etc. If so, do you know what proportion of detergent to water to use? Also, would this prove toxic to nesting and other young birds? And finally, what is a sure-cure, nontoxic method for dandelion purge (aside from the obvious hands-and-knees, dig-until-you-drop method)? Many thanks for whatever you can discover.

E. L., In the Garden

A: 1 teaspoon of liquid detergent added to 1 quart of water will make a spray that will be helpful in ridding plants and bushes of aphids, spider mites, white fly and thrips. It must be applied on the under and outside of the leaves every day for seven days (the life cycle of these pests). An even more effective organic spray, as it kills both eggs and pests, is as follows. Put 3 tablespoons dry, crushed hot pepper in ½ cup hot water. Let sit for half an hour. Strain. Mix with 1 tablespoon mineral oil and add to 1 quart liquid detergent spray. Don't use this mixture where birds are nesting or young are still in the nest, as red pepper is a powerful irritant; also, be careful not to breathe in the fumes while using it.

Whenever we spray with anything, we add ½ teaspoon per gallon of a miracle product called Basic H, which makes water 100-percent wetter by releasing its surface tension. Basic H is totally nontoxic, totally biodegradable and contains no phosphates. It is available through the Shaklee Home Products distributor in your area. They have no central lisiting in the state so, as with Avon, Tupperware and Amway, you'll just have to ask around until you find out who your distributor is.

For dandelions we think the best thing is to organically enjoy them: eat the young greens boiled or in a salad and use the blossoms to make dandelion wine!

READER FEEDBACK: A reader in Springfield wrote: "See *Folk Medicine* by D. C. Jarvis, M.D. and your troubles are over about tiny bugs, spider webs, etc. All I do is sprinkle a dusting of granite dust all over the plant and soil. And to take care of the dandelions just use a good pinch of lawn fertilizer containing US2 (Scott's, I think) in the center of the plant and a little on the blossom as soon as you see it."

BLISTER AND MILDEW

Q: Every year I seem to have the same trouble with my hollyhocks. They start in by being okay, and then they start getting blisters and rust, and some leaves wither and are terrible looking. It does not seem to affect the flowers, just the stalks and the leaves.

M., Rutland

A: We think your problem is caused by rust, a fungus disease brought into this country from France (via Chile) in 1886 on some infected seed. It has since spread throughout the country wherever hollyhocks are grown.

In the fall cut all your hollyhock plants to the ground. Burn the stalks, leaves and other refuse. Then next spring, as soon as leaves appear, dust with superfine sulfur and make subsequent applications every week or 10 days throughout the season. The following fall again cut down the plants and burn. The chances are you'll never get rid of the disease entirely, but you can at least keep it under control.

Q: I was treated to a stark surprise this morning. Every stalk of my phlox is covered with mildew. Checked my supply of Ortho products. None of them mentioned mildew or phlox. Obviously I do not own the correct product. Can you advise me how to get rid of this blight?

R. J. A., Poultney

A: The infecting culprit is a fungus called *Erysiphe cichoracearum* D.C. Its presence is not only disfiguring to the plant but will eventually be injurious to its growth. (So say the books, anyhow.)

To prevent its recurrence next summer, give the phlox a weekly dusting of sulfur. Now that the mildew has established itself, however, spray the plant with a wettable sulfur or Karathane (Mildex). Don't ever spray a fungicide containing sulfur if the temperature is 80 degrees or above, as the leaves may burn. Also, apply before it rains so that a protective coating will be present when the fungus spores start to grow in the presence of moisture. In the autumn when the phlox starts to die back, remove the tops from the plants and rake up and burn any fallen leaves.

Incidentally, we have never done any of the above. Our phlox have had mildew, we've slashed and cut them, divided and moved them at the wrong times and generally neglected them. Yet they've come back to flourish and multiply for the last 25 years.

Q: Can you tell me what is causing a whitish mold on the top of the dirt of some of my potted houseplants? I am wondering if it is a disease of some kind or perhaps something in the atmosphere.

N. S. M., Rutland

A: The "mold" you see on the top of your soil is actually a concentration of mineral salts, a result of watering frequently but not thoroughly. The mineral salts that normally occur in water are not flushed through, and they collect in the soil. Eventually the roots will become burned, and the plant foliage will become stunted and yellow. The solution to your problem is twofold. First take your plant(s) and fully immerse their pot(s) in lukewarm water for two to three hours. Stir the topsoil gently with your finger. This will loosen the salts and allow them to flush out. Second, in the future only water your plants every four or five days and soak completely until water comes out the drainage hole in the base of the pot.

SAVING OVER

Q: It's time to get my dahlias out of the ground, and I'm overwhelmed by choices presented to me by various gardening books as to the best way of storing the tubers. I know you can give me some hints.

Paraffin or Peat?, Windsor

A: Following the first frost (although we've often waited longer) cut the dahlia stalks off about six inches from the ground. Wait 6 to 10 days before digging to allow the tubers to "ripen." As the tuber clump can be up to a foot in diameter (spade up carefully), shake off any loose soil and turn upside down. Let sit for several hours so any excess sap and moisture can run out of the stalk. Store the tubers in a dry place where the temperature is, ideally, between 45 and 55 degrees. We put them in a garbage bag filled with peat moss and sand and stick them in a corner of our cellar. (Note: Store in a cellar, not basement: the cellar's dirt floor keeps the temperature at 55-65 degrees winter and summer.) The peat moss and sand aren't absolutely necessary. They just keep the tubers from shriveling.

In the spring moisten the peat and sand in the garbage bag a week or 10 days before planting. Buds will form, and you can then select the tubers with the healthiest growth. Divide the tubers: if there are no buds as yet, make sure each subdivision includes part of the neck, as it is from the base of this area that the buds will form.

Q. I've never seen you answer the question of how to save over geraniums. I do remember they're not to keep on growing, as they need a rest period, but what does one do?

J. K., Woodsville, New Hampshire

A: Given enough water and light, geraniums will keep blooming all year around. We usually dig them out of the garden the first week of September, making sure that when we dig them we take a circumference of soil equal to the diameter of the plant. This minimizes damage to the geranium's extensive root system. We don't bring the plant indoors right away but leave it on the porch for a couple of weeks to let it get used to its new pot. During this time we also pinch it back if it's looking weedy. Don't worry if you have to pinch off some stalks that have buds on them, new ones will come to take their place. The two most important things in wintering over geraniums are that they not be overwatered and that they have as much direct sunlight as possible. In our north country this means they should be put in a south-facing window. Even then you may not get blooms until February, when the days have begun to lengthen. Without sufficient light, they'll get stalky and start to yellow, and they won't produce any flowers.

We also grow geraniums from seed. They should be started in February for summer bloom: oddly enough, these do not seem to winter over as well as the "bought" varieties.

BULBS

Q: I have several bulbs I got this fall—tulips, crocuses, daffodils, etc.—that I did not have time to get planted. What to do? Is there any way to save them till next year?

W. H. M., White River Junction

A: You have two options. You can either force them for flowering four months from now, or you can keep them over and plant them in the spring.

Keeping Over: In the middle of January, or 12 to 14 weeks before your garden soil is workable, line a box or some other container with plastic and fill with 10 inches of potting soil (or soil from your garden, if you can still get at it). Plant the bulbs at the depth specified on the package: six inches is usually the depth for larger bulbs such as tulips or daffodils. Make sure the soil is moist but not wet. You don't need a particularly large container; as the bulbs are not taking any nourishment from the soil, they can be crowded together. The important growth that will be taking place over the next 12-14 weeks is in the root system, and the bulbs use the food they have already stored.

The bulbs have to be kept in a place between 35 and 45 degrees. Any colder and they will freeze; any warmer and they will start putting forth green nonproductive growth and will never flower.

We put the bulbs in the darkest and farthest corner of our dirt-floored cellar, up against the stone foundation. As soon as the ground in your garden can be worked in the spring, separate the bulbs out and plant them. They should flower right on schedule.

Forcing: Half-fill a container at least twice as deep as the bulb to be planted with equal parts of sand, peat and potting soil. Place the bulbs on the soil so their tips are just below the pot rim and add remaining soil till only the tips of the bulbs are visible. Water well and place in a completely dark, cool (40-50 degrees) place for at least 12 weeks until root, stem and bud develop.

During this time keep the soil well watered but not soggy. When the roots are visible through the drainage hole of the pot, place in a 60-degree, semidark area. After four days, transfer the pot to a well-lit, warm (60-70 degrees) place.

Warmer temperatures will shorten the blooming time. Full sunlight is best. After the plants have dried back, cut off the tops, place the bulbs in peat moss and store in the cellar for planting in the fall.

PLANTING AND TRANSPLANTING

Q: Our sidewalk is being moved, and as a result, we must move some azaleas and rhododendrons. Will it damage the bushes if we transplant them now (late May)? How do we do it, and what's the best time to move them if we ever have to do it again?

A Rhodie Lover, Montpelier

A: It's fine to move azaleas and rhododendrons any time. It is, however, very important to take a good root ball when you're digging up the plants and very important also to transplant at the same root level. Fill in the hole with good, loose dirt and add some peat moss and/or compost. Aftercare is equally important. Water generously twice a week if it doesn't rain, and mulch the plants with pine needles or shredded bark, as these two plants do well in acid soil.

Incidentally, we are cavalier about transplanting just about any bush or perennial: we move things around spring, summer and fall, although we usually do avoid digging things up while they are blooming. The two things to remember are a good root ball, and lots of water. If whatever we've moved doesn't seem to like where it is, we just dig it up and move it again. We haven't killed anything yet!

Q: I have a question I hope you can answer. There is a wild flower called lupus. They have beautiful blossoms and also produce their own seeds. I have transplanted a few, and they are now starting their seed pods. What I'd like to know is, could the seeds be put away and planted in the spring? We are thinking of moving, and I'd like to take some of these lovelies with me.

J., Hardwick

A: We think you mean *Lupinus*, more commonly known as "lupine." (Lupus is a disease.) Lupine may be readily propagated from seed: when the seed pods have formed remove from the stalks and then remove the seeds from the pods. Store the seeds in a dry place. Before you sow them, coat the seeds with a nitrogen-fixing-bacteria powder, the same stuff that is used on peas (lupine belongs to the same family). You can buy it any place that carries garden supplies.

You don't say where you are moving, but if it's any place that's hot and dry you probably won't have any luck growing lupine. Like peas, they need cool weather and a lot of moisture in both the soil and the atmosphere. The seeds of these lovely flowers, which originally came from England, have "escaped" the boundaries of cultivated gardens to grow in fields and along sunlit roads in northern New England.

Q: Why don't my two peony plants bloom? They are 4 to 4½ years old. They look healthy but have never had a bloom.

Maria Belanger, Montpelier

A: There are any number of possible reasons, but the three likeliest possibilities are: 1.) not enough sun. If the peonies get morning but no afternoon sun, they might as well be in full shade. Afternoon sun is best, because it is strongest, but full sun is preferable. (Our rule of thumb with all perennials; if they don't like where they are, dig them up and move them.) 2.) Not enough fertilizer. Peonies are heavy feeders. Make the first application of 5-10-5 or some other complete fertilizer early in the spring when new shoots are about a foot tall. Make the second application when the plant has finished blooming. 3.) The bushes were originally planted too deep. More failures with peonies are due to planting too deep than to any other cause. The eyes (or tops of buds) should only be 1 ½ inches below the surface of the soil. In the fall dig them up and raise them to their proper depth.

PRUNING

Q: We have two forsythia bushes some distance apart in our yard, and neither of them have blossomed in full for the three years. They have a few scattered blooms on the outer branches this year. Can you tell me why this is and if there is something that can be done to bring out the blossoms next year?

Andrew Currier, Brandon

A: You don't mention if you've been pruning your bushes. Forsythia requires pruning immediately after blooming. Several of the oldest stalks should be cut a few inches above ground level to allow new growth to take their place. If your bushes haven't bloomed very much for three years, your pruning should probably be pretty drastic; 20 to 25 percent of the branches should be removed. Prune the oldest and woodiest ones. If you neglect to prune the bushes every year, they will bloom only at the tips of some branches and begin to look unruly in the bargain.

Q: I have a three-year-old mock orange bush. It produced lovely clusters of flowers the first year, but the past year has put out only two or three flowers. Is there something I should feed it? Would fall be the best time? It is in partial shade and has grown tall and full. Should it be cut back?

M. B., White River Junction

A: Take heart: your mock orange will probably bloom this coming spring. When you bought the bush, the buds were most likely already established, and so the first year you had a lot of bloom. Mock orange hates to be transplanted, however, and takes two or three years to recover. Unlike some flowering bushes, they also resent being pruned except of their dead wood, and are much happier when left alone. If you should feel at some point that the bush is growing too big, thin it out during the winter by cutting the old branches as close to the ground as possible and the remaining branches by as much as a third. It will reward your care by refusing to bloom the following spring.

The nice thing about mock orange is that once it is established (as yours now seems to be) and healthy, the best thing you can do for it, other than cutting out the dead branches, is ignore it.

SEEDS

Q: I want the address of a coffee bean grower. I have written to Maxwell House and Folger's and haven't got an answer from either. I'd like a few coffee beans to grow a coffee plant. They have to be untreated and unroasted, obviously. Can you find an address for me?

J. B., Hardwick

A: We found seeds for coffee plants in the Park Seed Co. Catalogue. They are called *Coffea arabica*: "quick growing with shiny green oval leaves and red berries. Ten seeds for 95 cents." To receive a catalogue, write Park Seed Co., Cokesbury Rd., Greenwood, SC 29647.

Q: We have been looking for some spinach seeds that don't blossom at the first sign of warm weather. Can you help?

M. T. Alexander, Rutland

A: We have had terrific luck with a spinach called Fabris, from the Harris Seed Co. It is described as "extra-longstanding" in the catalogue, and it takes longer to bolt than any other kind of spinach we've ever grown. Order from Harris Seeds, Joseph Harris Co. Inc., Moreton Farm, Rochester, NY 14624.

Q: I have just built a small solar greenhouse and am looking for rare and wonderful seeds to plant that will survive in Vermont. Are there any seed catalogues that will tell me what I can and can't attempt and that also have interesting things to plant?

Ready in Barre

A: If this is your first year of growing things you are going to have to experiment. There are a great many variables at work, such as the quantity of available light and the mean temperature of your space. Here are addresses of two seed companies that have wonderfully exotic seeds: we've had great luck with them. Le Jardin du Gourmet, Box 48, West Danville, VT 05873, imports seeds from Europe and can furnish you with such delicacies as flageolets, haricots verts, petit pois, mache, arugola, radicchio and much more. Recipes are also supplied, in case you can't figure out what to do with what you've grown. Le Jardin's catalogue also has the most comprehensive list of herb seeds we've ever seen anywhere. J.A. Demenchaux Co., 827 North Kansas, Topeka, KS 66608, has been in business for many years and has some seed varieties you won't find anywhere else! We also recommend James U. Crockett's book, *Greenhouse Gardening* (Time/Life Encyclopedia of Gardening, 1977). We have found it more helpful than most books.

Q: We recently bought a house whose previous owner had a vegetable garden, and I plan to use the plot. This will be my first experience of growing vegetables, and I wondered if you could recommend a good how-to book and also tell me what seed catalogues would be good to use.

Looking Forward to Spring, Brownsville

A: We have two favorite "how-to" books on gardening which, despite being avid gardeners for years, we turn to frequently for reference and good ideas. They are both copiously illustrated and well indexed. The first is Dick Raymond's *The Joy of Gardening* (Garden Way, $21.95); the second is *Crockett's Victory Garden* (Little Brown, $9.95).

Crockett's book is divided into the 12 months of the year: each month tells you what and how to plant, about soil preparation, harvesting, storage, etc., in a particular month. His gardens were in the Boston area so, as a Vermonter, you'll want to move Crockett's timetable around a bit. He plants things in April that it would be unwise for us to put into the ground until the end of May.

Raymond, on the other hand, is a Vermonter and bases his timetable accordingly. He also addresses concerns and questions that we northerners are bound to have and has come up with some great ideas to lengthen our growing season. He does not, as Crockett does, include information on flower growing.

Our favorite seed catalogues are Johnny's Selected Seeds, Albion, ME 04910, and Vesey's Seeds, P.O. Box 9000, Houlton, ME 04730-0829. Both companies grow seeds that best withstand northern growing conditions. Johnny's will be particularly helpful to you as a new gardener: it is jam-packed with useful information on everything from soil temperatures to growing-schedule charts and includes a helpful system of coding that tells one, among other things, the best and most fool-proof variety of seed for beginners.

CUT FLOWERS

Q: Do you know of any homemade solutions that will prolong the life of cut flowers?

Wilting in Elmore

A: We have a brew that really does extend the life of cut flowers. Mix one part water, one part light-colored soft drink such as 7-Up and a few drops of chlorine bleach.

HOUSEPLANT WATERING

Q: I recently bought a house with a large solarium and want to fill it with plants. I'm concerned because there is a water softener in the house, and I wonder if a winter spent watering my plants with softened water will be harmful.

L. N., Norwich

A: First make sure both your hot and cold water run through the softener. The chances are the cold water doesn't. If your cold water is, for some reason, softened, there is a good possibility that it will harm your plants, particularly those that require a light or a sandy soil. What happens when water is softened is that calcium and magnesium ions in the water are replaced by sodium ions. These tend to break down soil particles, compacting the soil and destroying its aeration and moisture-holding capacity. Also, using softened water will, over time, increase your soil's salt content. Your plumber would doubtless be able to bypass the softener for one cold water tap in your house.

A note of caution: don't water your plants with cold water. Try to have the water at room temperature to prevent the root fibers from going into shock.

NETTLES

Q: What gives nettles their stinging properties?

B. J. C., Londonderry

A: The hairs of the nettle secrete a liquid containing formic acid, which is also present in the venom of biting ants. The best remedy for nettle and ant stings is an application of the juice of the jewelweed, also known as touch-me-not. Through history the nettle in infusion (teas, broths, etc.) has been used as a general tonic, a regenerator and purifier of blood, a diuretic and a stimulant for digestive functions. A 17th-century French abbot made this recommendation: "If you suffer from rheumatism that fails to respond to other remedies, beat or rub the affected area for a few minutes every day with fresh nettles. Your fear of this unusual rod will soon give way to joy as you feel your condition improving."

ROTOTILLER

Q: Does anyone make a small, reasonably lightweight electric rotary cultivator? It doesn't seem unlikely, but we haven't been able to find one. We are planning to have a small garden close to the house, and a small electric tiller would be perfect for us.

C. H., Brownsville

A: There is such a thing, at least at this writing, but they have apparently proven so unsatisfactory that hardware and equipment stores in our area are not going to carry them next year. They are lightweight, not very powerful and are more a cultivator than a tiller. We suggest you would be much happier with a Mantis Tiller Cultivator. It is gas powered, weighs only 20 pounds and does everything a big tiller would do if your garden is less than an acre. It comes with a variety of optional attachments. Write for a free brochure to Mantis Mfg. Co., 1458 County Line Rd., Dept. 775, Huntington Valley, PA 19006.

Soil

Q: I have a clay garden. It bakes down hard as a rock after each rain. Can you help me find an answer to my problem? I have tried adding sand and other material without success. Is there something I can do this fall to lighten the soil?

R. L. DeCelle, Waterbury Center

A: You need to add more organic matter, such as compost and manure. You might also have a load of topsoil or loam brought in. A perfect loam contains 40-percent sand, 40-percent silt and 20-percent clay. Thoroughly rototill in whatever you decide to use.

CHAPTER 12

RECIPES

The recipes our readers have sought and sent often delight us and sometimes make us gag. They certainly reflect the eclectic eating habits and culinary interests of Vermonters. The ingredients range from the natural—fiddlehead ferns that grow along our streams and river banks—to the totally artifical—boxed cake mixes and marshmallows. Our best hints for food preparation are scattered throughout this section. Happy eating!

HEAD CHEESE

Q: Do you know anyone who would have a recipe for old-fashioned head cheese? We make our own with sage, salt and pepper, but were wondering if there are other seasonings we can add?

S. and H. Root, Castleton

A: Paul Moeykens, of Windsor, gave Nan his recipe for head cheese, and it is superb. Nan's children and some of her friends are a little squeamish about head cheese. The kids are put off by coming home from school and finding pig heads boiling away in a giant kettle. So she calls her head cheese "pâté." It never lasts long.

After the meat has sloughed off the porkers' heads, Nan throws out most of the fat. She puts the meat, about 3 quarts, in a pot with 1 cup of broth that she has saved from boiling the heads. She simmers this and adds about 1 teaspoon of nutmeg, and ¼ teaspoon each of cinnamon and cloves. While this is simmering, she fries about 1 cup of onions until they are limp. She adds them along with salt and pepper to the meat mixture. She then grinds or mashes the mixture and puts it into a cake pan that has been cooled in the freezer for 20 minutes. It keeps well in the fridge or can be frozen.

CHEDDAR CHEESE SOUP

Q: I have fallen in love with a Canadian Cheddar soup that is seved at Carbur's Restaurant, in Burlington. Unfortunately, it's a long trip for a bowl of soup. I have checked many cookbooks trying to find the recipe, but I can't seem to find one that makes a creamy soup like Carbur's. The cookbook versions all have chunks of food in them.

No Name

A: We rang up Carbur's and had a nice chat with Brian, who kindly agreed to share the recipe. Although the restaurant makes it in 3-gallon batches, this recipe is for about ¾ of a gallon.

5 ounces roux	½ teaspoon celery salt
½ gallon milk	¼ teaspoon garlic powder
1 tablespoon sherry	¾ pound sharp Cheddar
1 teaspoon	cheese, grated
Worcestershire sauce	½ pound yellow American
½ teaspoon white pepper	cheese, grated

Make a roux by melting ½ stick of margarine in a saucepan and stirring in ⅔ cup of flour. Cook over low heat for five minutes, stirring constantly. Heat the milk in a double boiler and gradually add the roux with a wire whip. Add the sherry, Worcestershire sauce and seasonings. When the mixture starts to thicken, slowly add the cheese. Blend well. Simmer 30 minutes in the double boiler over low heat. Serve hot, garnished with bacon bits. Brian said the soup would hold for four days in the fridge, but it would not freeze successfully because the milk products would break down.

To avoid limp French bread you need first, a very hot oven (425–450 degrees) for the first 15 to 20 minutes of baking time. Second, make a firm and unshakable resolve not to open the oven door even a crack during that time. Third, secure a very hot brick and a pan of water that has been heated to boiling. You can heat the brick right on top of your gas or electric range. Set at medium heat, it will usually take 20 minutes to get really hot. When your oven is at temp and your bread ready to go in, put the pan of hot water on the bottom of the oven, and being very carful not to burn yourself, drop in the heated brick. Then quickly put the bread on the center rack of the oven and close the door.

It's the action of the steam and the high temperature that make the bread crusty; at the end of the 15-20 minutes take out the brick and pan and turn the oven down to 350 degrees and cook till bread is done.

RABBIT

Q: My husband went squirrel hunting and came home with a rabbit. It's cleaned and in the freezer. We're not into hasenpfeffer. Have you any ideas?

Hare, Manchester

A: This is one of our favorite rabbit recipes. Cut the rabbit into serving pieces and put it in a bowl. Pour over it the juice of 6 lemons, add salt and pepper and let it marinate for at least 12 hours. When it's time to cook it, pour about 1/4 inch of olive oil into a heavy pan and heat. When it's hot add a sliced onion, and when the onion is a bit brown add the rabbit. Brown on both sides and then add about 12 cloves of garlic. Don't be undone by the quantity of garlic, the final result is very subtle. Add more salt and pepper and about 1 cup of red or white wine. Cover the pan and simmer for 2½–3 hours.

> If you don't have ventilation above your stove you can eliminate smoke when you broil by putting water in the bottom of your broiler. It will absorb the smoke, and the fat from the meat will float, making for an easy clean-up.

TRIPE

Q: I would like to have a good recipe for coating tripe to make it nice and brown.

Doris Lezer, Corinth

A: Our food expert, Pat Baril, of Barre, said that her grandmother made the best fried tripe by just dredging it in flour and frying it in lard, quickly crisping it. If she was using pickled tripe, which has a lot of juice, she'd soak the juice up in a clean towel first. She sent us this recipe for crisp tripe.

1 pound fresh tripe	⅛ teaspoon pepper
1 egg	½ teaspoon dried sage
⅓ cup undiluted evaporated milk	1 small onion
	1¼ cups fine, dry bread crumbs
1 teaspoon salt	

Wash the tripe, cover with water, season with salt and pepper and simmer for about 1½ hours, or until tender. Drain and cool. Cut into pieces. Combine beaten egg, evaporated milk, salt, pepper, sage and onion. Dip tripe into mixture, then coat with crumbs. Arrange pieces on greased cookie sheet and let stand for 30 minutes. Bake in a preheated 400-degree oven for 20 minutes.

PEANUT BUTTER-BANANA LOAF

Q: During World War I our mother made a peanut butter-banana loaf, which was a substitute for meat. She baked it in a bread-loaf pan, and when ready to serve, she would slice it as you would meat loaf. There were, naturally, more ingredients than just peanut butter and bananas. My sisters and even my brother have tried to find this recipe through the years but have never found anyone who remembers the loaf. Perhaps you can find the recipe for me.

Anna L. Osborne, Rutland

A: We have pored through our vegetarian cookbooks and spoken to our always helpful Extension Service agent, all to no avail. Why don't you write The Peanut Advisory Board, P.O. Box 2329, Grand Central Station, New York, NY 10163, or Marilyn Hubert, Home Economist, Georgia Peanut Commission, 110 E. Fourth St., Tifton, GA 31794.

READER FEEDBACK: Several readers sent us recipes for peanut butter-banana loaf. The following is from Charles Griffith, of North Bennington.

2 cups sifted flour	2 tablespoons peanut
1 teaspoon baking powder	butter
1/2 teaspoon baking soda	1 cup mashed banana
1/2 teaspoon salt	1 cup chopped peanuts
1 egg, slightly beaten	
1 cup buttermilk or sour milk	

In a large bowl sift first four ingredients. Add remaining ingredients, mixing only enough to moisten. Pour into greased loaf pan, 9 by 5 by 3 inches, and cook at 350 degrees for an hour, then remove to rack and cool.

If you're having a large crowd of people over for a celebratory fish dinner, your dishwasher can double as a fish poacher. Take fillets of bluefish, cod, haddock or salmon. Lay on individual sheets of foil, dot with butter, sprinkle with shallots or scallions, lemon juice or thin slices of lemon and pepper. Wrap fish tightly, place on the top rack of your dishwasher and run at the hottest setting, full cycle. Make sure your water heater is set to 140 degrees. Dinner will be ready when the cycle is complete.

POLISH SAUSAGE

Q: I have been reading your column, and I would like a recipe for Polish sausage. I make Italian sausage for my own use, and I would like to make Polish sausage for Easter. Could you find me a recipe?

Clarence Edmunds, Rutland

A: Here's a recipe for fresh Polish sausage (kielbasa).

10 pounds of boneless pork butt	1 tablespoon coarse black pepper
6 tablespoons salt	1 heaping teaspoon of marjoram
1 tablespoon sugar	1 pint ice water
2 large buds fresh garlic	

Grind all the pork butts through a 1/4- or 3/16-inch grinder plate and place in your mixer. Add all the other ingredients and mix well, until all the spices are evenly distributed. Put into the stuffer using 40- to 42-millimeter hog casing. Put the finished sausages on an oven rack or bread-cooling rack and put this in the fridge where they'll dry. Be sure that you are using meat that has been chilled to between 30 and 34 degrees and that all the blood clots, bones, cords, etc., have been removed.

To prevent hamburgers from sticking to your barbecue simply take the grill off until you're ready to cook. If the grill is hot when you put your hamburgers (or whatever) on it, the meat will instantly cook onto the grill's surface. If the surface is cool, the meat, generating its own fats and juices, will have greased itself by the time the grill has heated up.

GROUND ARTICHOKES

Q: How does one prepare ground artichokes for eating? When prepared, how are they cooked? Boiled, baked or fried? The ground artichoke seems plentiful in this area.

E. Breset, Waterbury

A: How funny that you should ask! The ground artichoke (or Jerusalem artichoke, sun choke or *Helianthus tuberosis*) has been the bane of our life for years. We've done everything to get rid of it short of blowing it up. Since it will always be with us, however, we have also made a study of ways to use it, and there are almost as many as there are tubers in the garden. Incidentally, dig them early in the spring or wait until after the first hard frost.

Slice the tubers raw for a salad and serve with an oil-and-vinegar and garlic dressing, or oil them and roast in the oven alongside lamb, beef, chicken or pork. Slice and fry them as you do turnips or make a hearty casserole out of 4 cups peeled, boiled and mashed artichokes, 2 cups fine bread crumbs, 1/2 cup melted butter, 2 beaten eggs, salt and pepper to taste. Cook in a 350-degree oven for 30 minutes. You can boil them and serve them with a tasty Cheddar-cheese-and-cream sauce or use them mashed as a thickener for soups. You can make pickles out of them or use them in relishes and chutneys. You can even make a chiffon pie out of ground artichokes, according to one enthusiast. (We wouldn't touch that with a stick.) Incidentally, they are extremely nutritious and excellent for people with high blood pressure or diabetes. They don't keep well, however, as they have a fairly high water content.

If you come upon a slew of wild leeks while you're out on a walk, a fine way to preserve them, for spaghetti sauce or anything that calls for garlic, is to dry them. Put the leeks in a steam basket and steam for about six minutes. Remove the coarse part and cut them in half. Spread them out on a clean, nongalvanized screen, and leave them in the air or sun to dry. When they're crumbly they're dry. Store in airtight plastic storage bags in a cool, dry place.

TOO MANY TOMATOES

Q: I've canned as much of the tomato crop as I want and have been making sauce as well, but the more I think about it, the more it seems to me that one uses up an awful lot of expensive energy in the process of boiling to sterilize and boiling to thicken. Do you have any hints?

Tomatoed-Out in Tunbridge

A: Canning tomatoes is an energy-intensive process, although it's much less so if you have a pressure cooker. Here's a hint on how to save energy when you're making sauce. Take your tomatoes (raw and unpeeled) and put them through a food mill or a Squeez-O. Pour the resulting juice into a one-gallon plastic milk container, filling to just the bottom of the handle, and freeze. The night before you want to make tomato sauce, take the jug out of the freezer and suspend it upside down over a pot. The pot needs to be smaller in diameter than the milk container so the gallon jug is indeed suspended. In the morning you'll find about a quart of clear water in the pot and rich, thick tomato puree in your milk container. A friend simply puts her tomatoes on a cookie sheet directly into the freezer. Once they're frozen she puts them in a bag and defrosts them as needed.

To freeze rhubarb just wash the stalks, cut it up and put it on cookie sheets in the freezer. When it's frozen put it in freezer bags.

LEA & PERRINS BARBECUE SAUCE

Q: Years ago I tried a recipe for a chicken barbecue sauce put out by the good people at Lea & Perrins. I've lost the recipe and ask that you prevail on your readers to share their recipe with a starving fellow Vermonter.

C. J. G., Northfield

A: P. Graves, of Springfield, kindly sent along the following recipe for The Original Lea & Perrins Barbecue Sauce. We've tried it, and it's superb.

2 cups water
½ teaspoon black pepper
4 tablespoons brown sugar
1 teaspoon garlic salt or
   2 cloves garlic, chopped
   fine

2 teaspoons salt
1 cup cider vinegar
½ bottle Lea & Perrins
   Worcestershire Sauce
Juice of 4 lemons
4 tablespoons butter

Bring water to a boil in a 2-quart kettle. Add pepper, simmer 5 minutes. Add brown sugar, stir until dissolved, add garlic, salt, vinegar, and stir. Add ½ bottle (about ⅔ of a cup) of

Worcestershire sauce, simmer for a few minutes, add lemon juice and stir while heating. Add the butter just before using. It's easier to make up this sauce in a large quantity. By omitting the butter, it will keep for weeks in the fridge. When ready to use, heat slowly with the butter. Leave the butter out altogether when barbecuing pork.

To serve eggs Benedict to several people, partially cook the eggs ahead. Coat the bottom of a skillet with a film of oil and pour in water to which has been added a drop or two of lemon juice or vinegar. Have a bowl of ice water ready. When the water in the pan just starts to simmer, gently add the eggs, 4 at a time. Do not, ever, let the water boil. The second the egg whites begin to congeal, lift the eggs out with a slotted spoon and put them in the ice water. This will cause the yolks to harden so the eggs can be easily handled and the whites will keep their shape. When the time comes to serve, drop them back into the simmering water for about one minute or until they are cooked to taste.

WHITE-WINE VINEGAR

Q: I'm looking for a recipe for white-wine vinegar. Can you help?
T. L. C., Corinth

A: Here's a recipe for fine wine vinegar. Use a white Burgundy or Bordeaux. Pour either leftover wine or a new bottle of wine into a clean glass jar and cover with a layer of cheesecloth to keep out dust particles. Store the jar in a dark, warm place (at least 60 degrees). The wine will turn to vinegar in several weeks. Keep adding wine as you use the vinegar. It's almost impossible to control the acidity of this vinegar, since it changes composition so often. Before you use it, taste to find if it needs thinning with water or strengthening with additional vinegar or lemon juice.

FIDDLEHEAD FERNS

Fiddlehead ferns grow along the banks of rivers and streams. They appear in the early spring and are actually the top of the very young ostrich fern. They are tightly furled and sheathed in a paperlike brown covering. They must be picked before they unfurl, as their leaves, like those of all ferns, are poisonous. They are a delicious vegetable and make a superior pickle. Cleaning them is tedious. We used to rub the paperlike skins off, but our readers gave us some much better methods.

Method 1. Put the ferns in a lettuce-washing basket or fine string bag. Hang the container on a branch or a clothesline and spray with a high-pressure garden hose.

Method 2. When you go fiddlehead picking bring along a wire-mesh minnow trap. When you've picked enough ferns to fill the trap about ⅓ full put the trap into swiftly moving water, a waterfall is ideal. The skins will float away.

Method 3. Place the fiddleheads on a large mesh screen. Nan has one that she uses to dry onions. Reverse your vacuum cleaner hose and blow the skins off.

FIDDLE DILLIE PICKLES

Clean and blanch the fiddleheads. To each pint canning jar add: 1 teaspoon dill, ¼ teaspoon hot cayenne pepper, 1 clove garlic. For 6 pints mix: 3¼ cups vinegar, 3½ cups water, 6 tablespoons pickling salt. Bring this mixture to boil and pour over fiddleheads that you've packed into the pint jars. Pack a lot of fiddleheads in each jar, because they shrink. Process 10 minutes, seal and wait 2 weeks to use.

ROSE-HIP JAM

Q: My father, Peter Berini of Barre, is very interested in getting a recipe for rose-hip *jam*, not jelly. If any of your readers can help us out on this we would be most grateful. We have written to General Foods and received only a recipe for jelly.

Maria Hybord, South Barre

A: Here's a recipe for rose-hip jam.

6 cups rose hips, halved and cleaned of seeds
1 cup crab apples or other tart apples, unpeeled and diced

1 small potato, scrubbed and grated
⅓ cup lemon juice
3 cups honey

Stir all ingredients together and cook at a rolling boil until mixture sheets off a spoon. Pour into hot sterilized jars and seal.

SUGARLESS STRAWBERRY JAM

Q: I would like to make strawberry jam using an artifical sweetener, preferably Nutrasweet, instead of sugar. So far I've been unable to find such a recipe. Can you help?

Mary O'Neil, Castleton

A: How about a recipe that calls for no sugar *or* artifical sweetener? Here's one that we like.

2 cups mashed ripe strawberries
4 teaspoons tapioca
1 envelope unflavored gelatin

½ cup unsweetened white grape juice
2 teaspoons fresh lemon juice

Wash and mash berries. Combine tapioca, gelatin, grape juice and lemon juice over medium heat, stirring until gelatin is completely dissolved. Add berries and bring to boil, stirring constantly. Reduce heat and simmer uncovered about five minutes. Cool and refrigerate or freeze. Makes about 2½ cups.

FRUIT ROLL-UPS

Q: My kids really like to snack on fruit roll-ups. They are great to pack in lunch boxes, but they are expensive. Have you a recipe for them?

M. B., Barre

A: What you call fruit roll-ups, also known as "fruit leathers," are simply fruit purees dried to a nonsticky and pliable texture. Nan has been making them for ages. You can save oodles of money and can use all kinds of fruit. Leathers will last a month or more at room temp, four months in the fridge and up to a year in the freezer. The basic instructions are:

Use very ripe fruit. Use a blender, food processor, food grinder or potato masher to reduce the fruit to a pulp. Add only enough liquid to blend. Some fruits blend better if cooked a little first, such as rhubarb, apples and peaches. The liquid that you add can be water, cider or juice. The puree should be about like thick applesauce. If thickening is needed, add apple (high in natural pectin), wheat germ, chopped nuts, pectin or unflavored gelatin. You can combine fruits, and Nan strains the seeds from the berry purees. Pour the puree onto plastic (bread bags for instance) and dry at about 110 degrees until you can peel the sheet off cleanly. If you have a gas oven the pilot light will do. Don't overdry: the leather should be chewy, but not stiff. Store rolled in plastic wrap. Label.

GOAT'S-MILK FUDGE

Q: I am looking for a recipe for goat's-milk fudge. I had some years ago, and it was very good.

Gerry Sherman, West Rupert

A: Kay Griggs of the Central Vermont Goat's Club, of Barre, sent us this recipe. It's from *The Incredible Goat Cookbook,* which is published by the New Hampshire Goat Association.

2 tablespoons butter
2 cups sugar
2 tablespoons
  Karo syrup

$\frac{1}{2}$ teaspoon salt
$\frac{1}{3}$ cup cocoa
$\frac{3}{4}$ cup goat's milk
1 tablespoon vanilla

Mix all ingredients except the vanilla together in a heavy saucepan. Cook to a soft-ball stage—235 degrees on a candy thermometer. Add the vanilla and pour into a pan to cool.

CATHEDRAL COOKIES

A reader's request for these no-bake cookies filled our mailbox with recipe cards.

1 cup ground nuts
  (walnuts and pecans
  were most frequently
  mentioned)
1 package chocolate chips
  (12 ounces)

1 stick butter or margarine
1 package multicolored
  miniature marsh-
  mallows (12$\frac{1}{2}$ ounces)
flaked coconut

Melt chocolate chips and butter or margarine over slow heat or in a double boiler. Cool, then add marshmallows and nuts. Shape into logs 1$\frac{1}{2}$ inches in diameter. Roll in coconut. Refrigerate. When thoroughly chilled, slice into desired width. These can be frozen and thawed quickly. Some of the variations we received called for adding Rice Krispies or 1 cup crushed vanilla wafers and 2 beaten eggs.

BLACK WALNUT COOKIES

Anyone who has a source for these nuts and the patience to crack them can make these fine cookies.

$\frac{3}{4}$ cup shortening
2 cups brown sugar
1 cup nuts
2 eggs
$\frac{1}{2}$ cup evaporated milk

3 cups flour
$\frac{1}{2}$ teaspoon salt
$\frac{1}{2}$ teaspoon soda
1 teaspoon vanilla

Mix and drop on greased cookie sheets. Bake at 350 degrees for about 10 minutes.

OCTOBER PUMPKIN DOUGHNUTS

Q: I'm looking for a recipe for pumpkin doughnuts as well as a recipe for apple-cider doughnuts. Can you help me find them?
A. Jeness, Chester

A: Shortly after receiving your letter we received a request from Alberta Kock, of Benson, asking for a pumpkin doughnut recipe too: we came up with recipes for squash doughnuts and whole-wheat doughnuts, but no pumpkin doughnuts. Then, as if in answer to our prayers, we got a letter from Patricia Baril, of Barre. "If you need any help with your food questions," she wrote, "I'd be glad to be a resource for you." We called her up. "We have this problem, we can't find a recipe for pumpkin doughnuts," we said. "No problem," Pat replied cheerily, and we received the recipe in the next day's mail.

Compliments of Charles and Eileen Roeder, October Pumpkin Bed and Breakfast Inn, East Middlebury.

1 cup sugar
2 1/2 tablespoons butter or
margarine
3 beaten eggs
1/2 cup milk
1/2 cup cooked pumpkin
(unflavored)

3 1/2 cups sifted flour
4 teaspoons baking powder
1 1/2 teaspoons salt
1/2 teaspoon pumpkin-pie spice
oil for frying (unflavored)

In a bowl combine sugar and butter. Add eggs and blend. Add milk and pumpkin. In another bowl, combine flour, baking powder, salt and pumpkin-pie spice. Add liquid mixture to flour mixture gradually, beat vigorously with each addition. Add a bit more milk if necessary. Knead, place on a floured board, roll out to 1/4-inch thickness, use a doughnut cutter to cut dough. Fry in deep fat maintaining 370-degree temperature. Drain on crumpled paper towels and sprinkle with Vermont maple sugar crystals. Yield: 35-40 doughnuts.

APPLE-CIDER DOUGHNUTS

1 large egg	1 teaspoon vanilla
3 tablespoons sugar	1 cup flour
1 teaspoon nutmeg	2 cups Bisquick
1/2 teaspoon cinnamon	1 cup apple cider

Beat egg, sugar, spices and vanilla well. Add flour, Bisquick and cider. Mix well and roll out on floured board. Knead for a minute and then place in a plastic wrap and chill for at least 2 hours. Roll out, cut and fry in oil or lard, making sure the temperature never goes above 375 degrees or under 365 degrees. Yield: 2 dozen.

COTTAGE-CHEESE PIE

Louise Boynton, of Chittenden, asked for a recipe for this pie, Our answer was dull. Fortunately our dear readers set us straight. Here's the most frequently sent recipe.

1 unbaked 8-inch pie shell	3/4 cup sugar
1 1/2 cups small-curd cottage cheese	1 teaspoon cinnamon
	1/2 teaspoon nutmeg
2 eggs lightly beaten	1/2 cup raisins

Bake pie shell in 375-degree oven while combining remaining ingredients. Pour cottage-cheese mixture into pie shell. Sprinkle top with additional nutmeg. Return to oven and bake until set, about 45 minutes.

If you want a substitute for fruit-flavored gelatin in a dessert recipe use one envelope (1 tablespoon) unflavored gelatin, 1/2 cup water, 1/4 cup sugar and 1 1/2 cups fruit juice.

MILLION-DOLLAR PIE AND PISTACHIO INSIDE-OUTSIDE CAKE

We are apparently among the very small minority of the population of Vermont who did not have the recipes for (indeed, had never heard of) the following items. We received 127 copies of the recipes, easily breaking the reader-response record formerly held by the answer to the question, "Where can one buy paper toilet seat covers?"

MILLION-DOLLAR PIE FROM AUDREY PROSSER, OF RUTLAND

⅓ cup lemon juice
1 can sweetened condensed milk (14 ounces)
1 No. 2 can crushed pineapple, well drained
1 carton of frozen whipped topping, thawed (8 or 9 ounces)

1 package cream cheese, softened (8 ounces)
1 cup chopped nuts, save some for garnish
1 large or 2 small (9-inch) pastry or Graham cracker crust pie shells, baked and cooled

Mix lemon juice and the condensed milk. Add pineapple, whipped topping and softened cream cheese. Mix well. Stir in nuts. Pour into pie shells and sprinkle with reserved nuts. Cut into small wedges, as the pie is very rich.

PISTACHIO INSIDE-OUTSIDE CAKE

1 package, 2-layer size, white or yellow cake mix
1 package Jello pistachio-flavor instant pudding

3 eggs
1 cup club soda
1 cup oil
½ cup chopped nuts

FROSTING

1 envelope Dream Whip whipped topping mix	1 package Jello pistachio flavor instant pudding
1½ cups cold milk	mix

Blend all cake ingredients in large mixer bowl, then beat 2 minutes at medium speed. Bake in greased, floured 10-inch bundt pan at 350 degrees for 50 minutes. Cool 15 minutes. Remove from pan and cool on rack. Split into three layers. Whip the frosting ingredients together until thickened, about five minutes. Spread about 1 cup of frosting between layers, spoon rest into center, chill. Garnish with chopped nuts.

NUTRITIONAL TIDBITS PRESENTED AS A QUIZ

Q: Are fresh-water mussels edible?

A: Yes. Mussels feed by pumping water through their systems and extracting nutrients as it passes through. Fresh-water mussels are, however, extremely tough and virtually tasteless.

Q: How do you reduce flatulence when you're cooking beans?

A: By cooking a little summer savory (an herb) with the beans.

Q: Is there any difference between refined sugar and "raw" sugar?

A: Only the price. "Raw" sugar isn't sold in this country. What we actually get is coarsely crystallized, refined sugar that has been coated with molasses.

Q: When cooking oil is reused for deep-fat frying do you end up with fewer calories than you would get from fresh, unused oil?

A: No. The calories in any kind of food neither increase nor decrease when the food is fried in used or fresh oil.

Q: Do you know what "Reg. Penn. Dept. of Agriculture" means on many food packages?

A: It means just what it says. States require food products to be registered with departments of agriculture or secretaries of state, and the state has to approve the sale of the product. Pennslyvania has a law that requires the statement, "Reg. (with the) Penn. Dept of Agriculture" to be printed on food products sold in the state.

Q: Are organic/natural vitamins used more effectively by the body than nonorganic ones?

A: No. All vitamins that contain 100 percent of their recommended dietary allowance work exactly the same in your body.

Q: Where can one find hulled corn?

A: Hulled corn is the same as hominy. Many brands are available at supermarkets. We learned this when we answered our favorite food letter, which follows.

Q: My father is 81 years old and is looking for some hulled corn in a can to eat as is and to put in pea soup. We used to buy it here in Rutland, but you cannot buy it any more. I was wondering, if they're still making it, where we could buy same?

Wilma Foster, Rutland

P.S. This is all he has on his mind.

CHAPTER 13

WHERE CAN I FIND...?

Over the years we have received repeated inquiries for a source of wicks for lamps and stoves and of replacement pieces for china. We reluctantly republish answers to these two questions at least four times a year, asking our readers to please clip the column if they think they will ever need the information. But now, with this book, we will never have to take up column space on either subject again, except to say, "Refer to our book. It contains every source you need."

AMPLIFIER FOR TV

Q: I am searching for some kind of electronic device for a slightly deaf person to use while watching TV so the rest of the family does not have to have ears hurt by the loud TV.

N. E., Perkinsville

A: A set of headphones that plug right into the TV is one solution. Although they don't amplify they do cut out extraneous noise. Your TV can be wired to accommodate headphones for about $30,

145

and headphones sell from $19 up. (You can buy cheaper ones, but they tend to distort the sound.)

READER FEEDBACK: We received an ad from Dan Potter, of Bellows Falls, for a product called Lite Ears. The ad states, "Lite Ears permits one person to listen to television and control their individual sound level while others can listen at a level they like." The cost is $79.95, and a free brochure is available by writing ALF Engineering, Inc., P.O. Box 99061, Stockton, CA 95209.

Fran Flanders, of Springfield, wrote to us about a device called Speaker Remote Control Box (by Audiotex, No. 30-6008) which is attached to the TV set. It has a long cord which allows a small box to be chairside. This box has a speaker and an earplug jack to channel sound direct to the listener's ear. She also mentioned a very sensitive earplug made by Vanco called Private Ear (2 PD-1) which allows for a wide range of adjustment.

CAMPFIRE TOASTER

Q: Do you have any idea where I can find one of those pyramid-shaped things which are used to toast bread over campfires? I've looked everywhere.

S. H., Plainfield

A: We found your toaster at L.L. Bean, Inc. in Freeport, Maine. Coughlin's Camp Stove Toaster holds four slices of bread and sells for $1.50. Coughlin's Double Toaster holds two slices and, being of heavier construction, is $3. Neither of these is in the L.L. Bean catalogues, so if you wish to order them call Customer Service (800-341-4341) and tell the person you are speaking with that the toaster in question is a store item.

FIVE-GALLON GLASS BOTTLES OR JUGS

Q: I need to find some five-gallon glass bottles or jugs. In this day and age of all things plastic, are there such things?

J., Johnson

A: Well, we said, chuckling to ourselves, of course there are! About 10 phone calls later, we were seriously begining to wonder. You were right. Everybody, even the bottled-water companies, uses plastic! Then it occurred to us that places that carry supplies for making wine and beer might still have glass bottles and we started poring through our old standby, the Yellow Pages. No luck in Vermont, so we tried Boston and finally found what you wanted. Beer & Wine Hobby, P.O. Box M, Melrose, MA 02146 (617-665-8442), carries five-gallon glass jugs for $19.95. We asked why they were so expensive, and the fellow we spoke with said it was because they just aren't made in this country any more. He has to import them from Europe (he wouldn't tell us where). "Plastic is really no good for wine, as it has tiny pinholes which allow the wine to breathe. Also plastic jugs can't be reused, as they retain the old flavors," he said. You can either send for Beer & Wine Hobby's catalogue or order direct. "We have the largest inventory of beer- and wine-making supplies in the Northeast," the gent proudly stated. They will send via UPS and charge your purchase on VISA or Mastercard or COD.

NAVAL JELLY

Q: Can you tell us where we can get naval jelly? It's the greatest to remove rust. It was used in the navy on rusty fittings but works well on other things as well as fabrics. It is a pink cream and did come in bottles.

Eleanor Martin, Topsham

A: We found naval jelly at our local hardware store and our local farm-supply store. Why don't you check those in your area?

PAPER TOILET-SEAT COVERS

Q: Can you find anyplace that sells paper toilet-seat covers to use when one travels? I'm sure with the herpes scare they would sell well.

Kate Cross, Sudbury

A: The smallest quantity we could find was at White River Paper in White River Junction. A carton of 2,500 covers costs a little over $31.

READER FEEDBACK: Our mailbox was jammed with replies. We received a lifetime supply of paper toilet-seat covers from our dear readers. It turns out that many mail-order firms carry them. Miles Kimball at 41 W. Eighth Ave., Oshkosh, WI 54906, was the most frequently mentioned and inexpensive source for this unexpectedly popular item.

SPRUCE CHEWING GUM

Q: I'm looking for commercial spruce chewing gum. Can you help?

Earle Ennis, Cabot

A: Kennebec Spruce Gum is made by the G. F. Carr Co., Five Islands, ME 04546, and is often available in the candy section of country stores.

SPOON HOLDER

Q: Help! I want to buy a spoon holder for at least 60 spoons. The holders go on the wall, but where can I find one? I know that Cape Craftsmen, Inc., make them, but I have no address for them. I hope that you can help me.

Verlie Vaughn, Proctor

A: The address for Cape Craftsmen, Inc., is P.O. Box 517, Elizabethtown, NC 28337.

BORAX

Q: Is borax still manufactured? I can't purchase it in any store. I'm not talking about borax hand soap: I mean pure borax.

O. P., Brandon

A: Borax, according to our dictionary, is sodium borate, a crystalline compound used to make glass, soaps, enamel and pharmaceuticals. Our grocer checked his most complete catalogue and couldn't find pure borax, nor could he remember its ever being sold. The gents at the feed store told us that *boron* is sold in 100-pound bags and is used for fertilizing the fields. Sorry we can't be of help. Readers, what do you know about pure borax?

READER FEEDBACK: The letters quite literally poured in. Here is a very small sampling.

Lillian Davidson wrote: "Borax can be found on most chain-store shelves. I am surprised your local grocer didn't find it listed: it was probably filed under 20 Mule Team 99½ percent Pure Borax. U.S. Borax and Chemical Corp., 1079 Wilshire Blvd., Los Angeles, CA 90017, is listed on the box as manufacturer. I find borax very useful in controlling crabgrass between stepstones on paths. I apply it once a year."

LaRoux Robertson, of Montpelier, writes that she remembers borax on her mother's laundry shelf: she uses it to dry flowers.

Mrs. C. Laundry, of Montpelier, writes, "I have an old box of 20 Mule Team Borax that is 40 years old or more. There's very little left in the box, which says it 'speeds and sweetens laundry.' It's a 1-pound box, and '16 cents' is stamped on it so I expect it cost 16 cents at First National."

Pat Stuart, of Northfield, sent along a side panel of 20 Mule Team Borax and said, "I read your column today and then dug up an old box of borax. I still had it on the shelf from when my kids were little. My youngest is 11 now, so I got this stuff to sweeten their diapers."

Hubbard Richardson, of Springfield, in a chatty letter, told us that "borax comes from Death Valley, California, and the company used to sponsor a TV program called 'Death Valley Days'."

Edna Atkins, of Barre, sent us an an almost-empty 20 Mule Team box and said, "Needless to say, I'm 85 years old. Think I used it to clean the refrigerator or milk bottles. This box is an antique, I guess. I have not used it for years but had it saved in the cupboard. Someday I'll clean house."

DUST PAN

Q: I am looking for a dust pan with a long handle, one you don't have to bend over to use.

Joyce, Barre

A: We have three catalogue sources for a long-handled dust pan and broom set. The first is Solutions, P.O. Box 6878, Portland, OR 97228, or call toll-free 800-342-9988. The second is Lillian Vernon Corp., 510 South Fulton Ave., Mt. Vernon, NY 10550. The third is Colonial Garden Kitchens, Unique Merchandise Mart, Building 66, Hanover, PA 17333. They also have a toll-free number: 800-621-5800. The price is uniformly $13 for the set (give or take a few cents). Incidentally if you are a gadget lover, we heartily recommend these three catalogues. They make great reading!

OAKITE

Q: Have you ever heard of a product called Oakite, which was marvelous for many things years ago—in my case, releasing the burnt-on food from my favorite saucepan? I have looked in vain for Oakite in supermarkets. No one has even heard of it. Perhaps it has been discontinued or has a new name?

B. B., Brandon

A: We remember Oakite occupying a prominent place in our kitchens when we were growing up. We haven't seen it for ages, either.

In checking around with various old timers like ourselves we found that Oakite hasn't been available in Vermont or New Hampshire for at least eight years. Before that it had moved from Household Goods into Paint Supplies, where it was recommended for washing walls. Although we've been unable to verify our assumption, we think Oakite was taken off the shelves because its phosphate content exceeded the limit set by environmental protection agencies in both states.

To clean burnt-on food, since you can't get Oakite, we suggest our old standby, dishwasher detergent (such as Calgonite). Make a strong solution with hot water, soak your pan overnight and presto!

Electric Butter Churn

Q: Do you know where I can purchase an electric butter churn? Wintertime is popcorn time, especially if it's topped with homemade butter. Also, homemade bread toasted on top of a kitchen wood stove deserves only homemade butter. I'm looking for a glass-jar type churn, a gallon or two.

Ed Wiggin, Mendon

A: A good friend makes wonderful butter with a glass-jar electric churn. She bought it out of a Sears catalogue: not the regular one but the Farm Equipment catalogue.

READER FEEDBACK: Philip C. Miller sent in this grand suggestion, which falls into the same category as our recipe for poaching fish in the dishwasher: "Many years ago my grandmother found herself in the position of having a lot of cream and no churn. Her solution was to securely tape a wide-mouth canning jar three-fourths full of cream to her washer agitator and run the washer without water until the butter was done. With modern washers the water would have to be shut off and the washer carefully watched so it didn't go into the spin cycle. If it did (go into the spin cycle) I wouldn't care to think about the results. For a jar I would recommend a one-gallon plastic mayonnaise jar, or smaller, depending on the amount of cream on hand. Either wide surgical tape or duct tape will work for securing the jar to the agitator."

Pancake Dispenser

Q: I am enclosing a newspaper clipping that has a picture of a pancake dispenser used by the Sugar and Spice Restaurant in

Mendon. I used to have one about 15 years ago and would like to know where I can purchase another.

Jack Deracleo, Poultney

A: Phil Moore, proprietor of the Sugar and Spice Restaurant, kindly gave us the name of his pancake-dispenser supplier. You can order the item from Dick Whitbeck Food Service Supplies, 24 Oakwood Place, Delmar, NY 12054. The phone number is 518-439-6366. He noted that the two dispensers he bought three years ago are approaching a million pancakes apiece! (Eat your heart out, McDonald's.)

SOAPSTONE SKILLET

Q: My mother, who lives out of state, has asked me to find a soapstone skillet for her. I have tried hardware stores in the area, also What's Cooking in Barre, but no luck. Hope you can help me.

A Montpelier Reader

A: We called the Vermont Soapstone Company in Perkinsville. The lady we spoke with said that while they make soapstone griddles, they don't make skillets. She said she's received calls in the past from people looking for skillets but has told them what she told us: she's never heard of a soapstone skillet being made by anyone—the labor involved in hollowing out a piece of soapstone to make a skillet would be prohibitively expensive.

Vermont Soapstone *griddles* are sold throughout the state. They can also be ordered from Orton's Country Store, in Manchester.

"SUGAR-STIRRING" PANS

Q: Our church in East Corinth uses old (antique, really) "sugar-stirring" pans for their Old-Fashioned Chicken Pie suppers. Several of these old pans need retinning. We have been unable either to find a place where we can have this done or to find a source for new pans of a similar or preferably slightly larger size. Our good neighbors in Bradford have been generously lending us their pans used for their famous game supper. These too are quite old and seemingly irreplaceable. Can you help us?

East Corinth Congregational Church

A: We couldn't find a source for the pans (faithful readers, can you help?) but you can have them retinned by The Tinning Company, 69 Norman St., Everett, MA 02149 (617-389-3400).

READER FEEDBACK: Peter Moore, of Windham, wrote: "You asked that a faithful reader help you find a source for tinned pans of a special dimensions. I suggest you try ABKO Metal Mfg. Co., 525 W. 26th St., New York, NY 10011. This excellent concern makes, among other things, scale scoops, oat measures, pullman pans with covers and drip pans to use under fire engines when garaged. The company made us tinned English muffin rings, which we had not been able to find elsewhere. They will also retin breadbuckets. Call 212-244-4896 and ask for Miss Miles, owner and CEO. She will help you."

GUARDIAN SERVICE LID

Q: I have been unable to locate a glass lid for a cast-aluminum canning kettle. It is marked "Guardian Service" on the bottom. I would appreciate any information concerning a possible source for a replacement lid.

Norma Sposta, Pittsford

A: You can get a replacement lid from Don Stevenson Co., Mail Order, 2727 E. Dutch Ave., Anaheim, CA 92806. When you write them, be sure to include the dimensions of your kettle.

LIFETIME STAINLESS STEEL

Q: I have a Lifetime Stainless Steel pan that needs a knob and a handle replaced. I wrote to the parts' makers, in Framingham, Massachusetts, and in LaGrange, Illinois, but both letters were returned. Can you help me?

Sylvia, Barre

A: Lifetime is made by the West Bend Corporation. You can write to them Attention: Customer Service Department, Lifetime Stainless Cookware, 400 West Washington St., West Bend, WI 53095 (414-334-2311). Ask them for the name of their representative in your state.

REVERE WARE

Q: I have a Revere Ware saucepan, but it's hard to use because the plastic knob fell off the cover and was lost. Do you have their address so I can write for a remedy? Also, the pan has mineral deposits inside. What's your home remedy for this?

A. T. C., Cabot

A: The address for Revere Ware is Revere Copper and Brass, P.O. Box 250, Clinton, IL 16127. The phone number is 217-935-3111. When you write them, why don't you ask them what home remedy the firm recommends for the removal of mineral deposits? By the way, when we were in the library doing some research on an entirely different subject, a gent there told us that his wife cleans the copper bottoms of her Revere Ware pots with catsup, and it works like a charm!

WEAREVER STEAMER

Q: We have a very old four-part steamer. The bottom has given up the ghost, and it's too old to repair. Perhaps if I could write to Wearever they could give me an idea of another of their products that would work or, better yet, find one in the attic and send it to me! Can you find me their address?

Bob McCorckle, Williamstown

A: We talked with Camille Zampetti at Wearever's regional office in New Jersey: she told us the company is no longer making steamers of any kind. She had, however, on the very morning we called, just come from a meeting where the possibility of going back into production had been discussed. She thought the best thing for you to do was write the main office: Consumer/Public Relations, Wearever-Proctor Silex, 1089 Eastern Ave., Chillicothe, OH 45601, or Customer Service, same address (614-773-9100).

CHINA AND CRYSTAL

Q: I would like to secure the name of a firm that deals in out-of-date china and crystal patterns. I have seen their ads in magazines but have never clipped the addresses. I would like to secure a couple of pieces of Royal Jackson china and Fostoria Teardrop crystal that have broken over the years.

Ruth Smith, Barre

A: The above is only one example of the many letters we have received over the years asking for addresses of china and crystal replacement companies. Below is a list of those we have heard are the most helpful and reliable.

Locator's, Inc.
708 Rock St.
Little Rock, AR 72202
(501-371-0858)

This firm stocks, buys, sells, and brokers discontinued patterns of china, glass and silver. They keep an extensive registry of names linking buyer to seller, and vice versa. If they don't have the pieces you want, for a fee of $3 they will put your name in their registry and keep it until they locate a match. Write them giving the name of manufacturer, pattern and a description of the pieces you want replaced and enclose an SSAE envelope for their reply.

Patterns, Unlimited
P.O. Box 15238-US/TX,
Seattle, WA 98115
(206-523-9710)

Patterns will hunt for replacement pieces for you. They will not only search for a match in china and crystal but in discontinued silver and earthenware patterns as well. Write them and tell them exactly what you want (make, pattern and model number if you have them), and include a business-size SSAE. They keep all requests on file until they are filled.

Replacements, Ltd.
1510 Holbrook St.
Greensboro, NC 27403-2785
(919-275-7224)

We have heard nothing but good things about these folks: we've been told they are extremely efficient, reliable and reasonable in price. They claim they are the world's largest service for replacement of discontinued crystal and china. Their literature says: "We maintain a constantly changing inventory of over 10,000 difficult to locate patterns." If they don't have what you want, they'll try to find it for you.

McCoy USA

Q: Could you find out for us the address of the firm that makes McCoy USA pottery? There is the number 7050 on the bottom of the cups we want to get replacements for.

George, Montpelier

A: The address is Nelson McCoy Pottery Company, P.O. Box 130, Lancaster, OH 43130.

SILVER

Q: I have lost one dessert fork of a Rogers and Brothers (1847) Lovelace pattern. I wonder if you could find the pattern for me.

M. W., Ludlow

A: We can't find it, but we'll bet you these people can: Rogers Sterling Matching Service, Dept. US, P.O. Box 1665, Mansfield, OH 44901. They have an 800 number so you can call them free: 800-537-5783.

Lamp Parts

Q: I have an old circular-wicked oil lamp. The glass chimney broke and I have not been able to find a replacement. The base of the chimney was 1½-inch O.D., and after 2 inches it tapers to 1 inch for the next 8 inches. None of the current replacement chimneys come close, and I've seen nothing in any catalogue. Hope you can help.

Tom Franks, Shaftsbury

A: Even with your good description, we are afraid we can't help you without the name of the manufacturer of the lamp, in addition to any other name or model number on any of the lamp's other working parts. We suggest you write or call Lehman Hardware and Appliances, Box 41, Kidron, OH 44636. Their telephone number is 216-857-2931. The firm specializes in old and discontinued stove wicks and lamp parts and has an enormous inventory. If anyone can help you, the Lehman people can. They are the ones we would have consulted for you had you included the necessary information.

Q: I have an old glass lamp that needs a new glass globe. Do you know where I can find one?

B. J., Brattleboro

A: Lamp Glass, 2230 Mass. Ave., Cambridge, MA 12138, stocks over 100 different sizes of glass lampshades and globes. Their phone number is 617-497-0770. If you have no luck there, you can try your luck at Lehman Bros. (see above).

Stove Parts

Q: I am writing for a neighbor. He'd like to know if you could tell him where he can find firebrick lining for an old stove. The lining is gone, and he can't find any around here. He lives alone. His stove is real old and is a Fairmount. Can you help him?

Mrs. J. E. Flynn, Roxbury

A: We weren't able to find any firebrick for your neighbor's stove, but we do have a suggestion. One of our stove experts said to use standard firebrick and then form the corners with Redi-Mix refractory cement. This combination, he said, will do the job. Montpelier Stove Works, 203 Barre St., Montpelier, VT 05602, carries the unmixed cement (cheaper than the Redi-Mix) and firebrick: they can also do the job for your neighbor. Their number is 802-229-0150.

READER FEEDBACK: Janet Martin, secretary of the board of the Rutland Fire Clay Co., wrote to let us know that the company started making stove lining in 1883 and is still selling it. The firm carries a complete line of stove products.

Q: I have a Crawford Anniversary Special wood cookstove with a hot-water font that has started to leak on the back side. This is an old stove, made in 1925, but in excellent shape. I wonder if you by any chance can tell me where these are made. There is a number A8-20 on the top of the stove.

R. R. Miner, Brandon

A: Sadly, the wonderful Crawford stove is no longer being made, but spare parts are available for it at Bryant Stove Works, Thorndike, ME 04986 (207-568-3663). Bryant is the biggest restorer of wood stoves in the country and it specializes in stoves made in New England. It stocks a big inventory of parts, and those it doesn't have it can make, as long as it has an old part to use as a pattern. If they don't have what you need to repair your water font, they will either know where you can go to get it fixed or they'll make something up for you that will remedy the problem.

Q: My combination gas-and-wood stove was made by the Florence Stove Co., in Gardner, Massachusetts. The part I need is the large cross member that is in the center of the wood-burning side. My stove model number is D 8960, and the serial number is 249717. I'd like to know what became of the Florence Stove Co. and where all the original parts went.

H. W. Yoos, Mt. Holly, New Jersey

A: The Florence Stove Co. is no longer in business. According to Clifford Porran, of The Midwest Antique Stove Clearing House and Parts Registry, the following sources may be able to help you: Macy's Texas Stove Works, 5515 Alameda Rd., Houston, TX 77004; Lehman Hardware & Appliances (mentioned above); and Dave Erickson, P.O. Box 2275, Littleton, MA 01460. He bought a large inventory of obsolete stove parts from Waverly Heating Supply Co., which used to have plenty of Florence parts in the 1930s. You could also write Midwest Antique Stove Clearing House and Parts Registry, 417 N. Main St., Monticello, IN 47960. Among other services the Clearing House distributes various pamphlets and reprints that cover a variety of subjects, from "How to Get Parts for Your Antique Stove" (which includes sources of ready-made parts) to "What Is My Antique Stove Worth?" The Clearing House also puts out a quarterly newsletter called "Stove Parts Needed." Send them an SSAE and ask them about the part(s) or patterns to reproduce the parts (which Bryant Stove Works will do for you: see address above) that you need.

STOVE WICKING

Q: I have a Florence combination oil-and-gas stove. I used to be able to get wicks in any hardware store. Now it's impossible to find them. All I can buy is wicking in rolls. We used to buy the wicks all made up for Florence burners, size 6 and 7 inches. They called them E-Z Lite Kindlers. There was a middle on the inside of the wicks that held them in place. The wicks in a roll won't stay in place. The last box I got was manufactured by the Asbestos Weaving Company, Clinton, Massachusetts. I would like to obtain some of these wicks. Can you help?

Margaret L. Flynn, Roxbury

A: The Asbestos Weaving Co. was bought out years ago by Perfection Products, in Waynesboro, Georgia. They in turn sold all the tool-and-die equipment needed to make your wicks to an Amish company in Indiana, which specializes in making wicks for old stoves and lamps. Their address is: Schwartz Mfg, Co., RR, Box

53A, Burne, IN 46711. You can also write Lehman Hardware and Appliance (address above) and ask for their catalogue. The store is owned by the Amish and they specialize in old and discontinued wicks, replacement parts for old stoves and lamps, nonelectrical hand tools, etc.

Q: I am looking for a tank and wicking for a rather old but usable Perfection Smokeless Oil Heater No. 230-C. Have tried local stores, and I'm unable to locate the above and have been told I probably can't. Can you help?

Beryl Medlar, Montpelier

A: Perfection Products, in Waynesboro, Georgia, still has parts and wicking for your oil heater, but unfortunately you can't order directly from the factory. They have no representative in Vermont, but when we called the company the lady in the parts department asked what other states were near us. (If we had said Alaska we don't think she would have blinked an eye.) She looked up various New England states (when we told her what their names were) and the nearest distributor for Perfection is S&M Distributors, Greenville, RI 02828 (401-949-3390). They'll order what you need.

Q: Can you tell me where, if anywhere, I can find wicks for the Kero-Sun Portable Heater? I bought a new one but can't find where the wicks can be bought, as I'm told the company has gone out of business. The stove is no good if I can't buy the wicks, as the fiberglass wick I can buy smells when the stove is lit. Also, I would like to find a lighter for it. I'm wondering if they're still making Kero-Suns as there are a number of those heaters around here.

No Name, Roxbury

A: Kero-Sun Heaters are still being made, and Boulevard Gardens, Barre-Montpelier Road, Barre, VT 05641 (802-479-2253), carries a complete line of them. They also have wicks and lighters—or "igniters," as they are actually called.

The smell from your heater has nothing to do with your fiberglass wick but rather is caused by impurities in the kerosene you are using. If kerosene has more than 0.3 percent sulfur in it, it's going to smell when burned. Unfortunately it's almost impossible to get really pure kerosene in Vermont. People won't buy it, as clear kerosene costs from 20 to 25 percent more than the impure stuff. Pure kerosene is absolutely crystal clear rather than cloudy. Another hint: kerosene kept over the summer should be stored in a dark place, as it will break down quickly when exposed, even indirectly, to the sun and will as a result burn inefficiently and eventually clog your heater.

ABRASIVE TAPE

Q: We have two old-fashioned bathtubs in our home. Several years ago we bought kits of self-sticking abrasive tapes that, pasted in the tub, provided a sure, nonslip surface. Now some of the tapes have smoothed down, while others have pulled off. It's necessary to get new ones, however all we can find are those cute little flower stick-on pieces, which are quite useless, as they are practically nonabrasive. Can you please help us find some of the original 1-inch-wide abrasive self-stick tapes?

Bill Kelmsley, Bellows Falls

A: We called hardware stores, plumbing suppliers, general stores, bath shops. No one had anything except flower stick-ons, although a number of people said they wished they knew where to get abrasive tape, as many of their customers had asked for it. And then we had an inspiration! Who, we thought, would derive the most benefit from these strips? Hospitals and invalids, was the answer. So we started calling medical-supply companies (look them up in your Yellow Pages under "Medical Supplies"). The tapes are available: strips are 1½ inches in width and are packaged in boxes of 8 and 12 strips. As of this writing they cost between $4 and $6 a box. Our local and ever-helpful resource, Keene Medical Supply, Lebanon, NH 03766 (603-448-5225), said they would be happy to order the tapes for any of our readers who called or wrote in.

ODD-SIZED CANDLES

Q: My wife and I have a pair of candle holders that take odd-sized candles. We've checked stores and specialty shops with no luck. Any idea where we can buy odd-sized candles, or have some made?

D. S., Barre

A: Colonial Candles, in Hyannis, Massachusetts, makes just about any candle, in any color, to fit any size holder ever made. There is probably a shop in your area that carries their line. If for some reason they don't carry what you are looking for, ask to see the Colonial catalogue.

There are a couple of tricks for making candles fit odd-sized holders. If your candle holder is too small, take the candle and immerse three inches of the candle base in boiling water. (If you dip just the end in, the candle will crack.) Then insert into holder, wiping away the excess wax.

If the holder is too large, Colonial Candles makes a nifty little item called Candle Stix. They are small, tallowy, ovoid disks that come 15 to a package. You put one in the bottom of the candle holder, and it holds the candle firm.

CEDAR OIL

Q: I would like to know where to buy cedar oil, as I have a closet that I would like to paint with it.

Neil McRae, Barre

A: We pulled a blank: all we could find was cedar-oil spray, which is available from The Vermont Country Store, Mail Order Office, P.O. Box 3000, Manchester Center, VT 05255 (802-362-2400). It costs about $11 a pint.

READER FEEDBACK: A reader who wished to remain anonymous sent us the following: "You can get cedar oil from George C. Brown & Co., Inc., Greensboro, NC 27400. It's called Brown's Supercedar

Oil of Cedarwood, and it was about $10 a quart a few years ago. It's not a spray: you can brush it on to restore the odor in cedar closets. I also used it to try to make cedar incense (without success) although it worked very well in my wife's cedar closet." The gentleman didn't send us a street address for Brown & Company but we got the phone number from Information: 919-292-2961.

PLUMBING FIXTURES

Q: Do you have any idea where I could purchase a top-mount 3 1/2-inches center faucet for a cast-iron bathtub?

No Name, North Springfield

A: Renovator's Supply, Miller's Falls, MA 01349, might carry them. Write for their catalogue or give them a call at 413-659-2211. Antique plumbing parts are nearly impossible to find. Salvage yards rarely have them because they wear out before the fixtures. Reproductions are the only solution.

REPLACEMENT LINE FOR GRASS TRIMMER

Q: Please help me find the precut replacement line (Number 82-101) for my Black and Decker grass trimmer.

P. M., Lake Bomoseen

A: We get about ten requests for Black and Decker replacement line every summer! You can use any 50-foot-long, 0.065-inch-diameter precut trimming line, available wherever lawn-and-garden equipment is sold, also in most hardware stores. You'll have to wind it on the spool yourself (a very simple procedure). Or you can order the line from Black and Decker, Grass Trimmer In-Pack Offer 11, P.O. Box 171, Hampstead, MD 21074. It's catalogue No. 82-101.

WALLPAPER BY MAIL

Q: I am looking for companies from which to order wallpaper by mail. I am hoping you have readers out there who have done this and have been very satisfied as to quality and price.

Shirley Hartson, Calais

A: Robinson's Wallcoverings, Dept. 277, 225 W. Spring St., Titusville, PA 16354, carries an extensive selection of wallpapers at discounts of up to 50 percent. Their merchandise is made for them by leading manufacturers but sold under their own label. Send them $1, and they'll send you their catalogue.

READER FEEDBACK: Rose Anne Cummings, of Arlington, wrote: "I heartily recommend Sharp's Wallpapers Inc., Bridgeton-Fairton Rd., P.O. Box 237, Bridgeton, NJ 08302 (800-257-7030). Many of my friends have been ordering from this company for years and have been very satisfied with the selection, quality and service."

WILKINSON SWORD PRUNING SHEARS

Q: My problem is a broken spring on a pair of Wilkinson Sword pruning shears. I'm sure they would still be good if I could replace the spring. I've asked at hardware stores, and they have no answer.

Sally Elliot, East Dorset

A: We suggest you write directly to Wilkinson Sword, Inc., 7012 Best Friend Rd., Doraville, Atlanta, GA 30362. If there is a number of any kind on your shears, be sure to include it in your letter.

CHAPTER 14

UNCLASSIFIED INFORMATION

This chapter represents the quintessential *Ask Anne & Nan*—a little bit about a lot of things. The information here defies classification and delights us. Do you know how to repair rubber gloves? how to preserve newspaper? how to make a Depression garden? Neither did we until our dear readers asked.

CREMATION INFORMATION

Q: We are a couple in our eighties, so we know that before too many more years, the bell is going to toll. We would both like to be cremated in as simple packaging as is permissible. We feel that it is foolish and wasteful to buy expensive coffins to be burned up. Will you please advise us on how to arrange things?

Name withheld

A: We called several crematories around Vermont and discovered that one allows reinforced-cardboard containers but charges much more for the actual cremation than another place which requires a wooden container. The gent in charge at the Mt. Pleasant Crematory, in St. Johnsbury, explained that the reason for requiring a wooden container is that it allows crematory personnel to handle a body in the most decent and dignified way. He said a cardboard container is unsatisfactory especially if the deceased is heavy.

Some crematories have programs which allow you to prearrange and prepay your cremation. Look in the Yellow Pages under "Crematories" and call several and shop around for the firm that is best able to meet your needs.

SEED TEETHING RINGS

Q: I would like to know the name of a type of teething ring that was used over 70 years ago. They were light gray and sort of pear-shaped, shiny and very hard. Some have told me that the rings were some kind of seed that was dried and strung.

O. G., Montpelier

A: The beads are known as Job's Tears, a seed of the grass Coix lacryma-jobi of tropical Asia. These seeds were used as necklaces for teething babies. They were popular at the turn of the century but fell from favor when it became apparent they could break and cause a baby to choke. The seeds for this ornamental are listed in the W. Atlee Burpee catalogue, 300 Park Ave., Warminster, PA 18991.

DANGER FROM HANDLING ANIMAL SKULLS

Q: On walks in the woods, I sometimes find interesting objects such as animal skulls. If an animal whose skull I found happened to die from rabies, is there danger from handling the skull? Would bringing it home in a plastic bag and soaking it in boiling water and bleach destroy any remaining germs?

Unsigned, Montpelier

A: According to a doctor in the Pathology Department of Animal Health, a division of the Animal Science Department, University of Vermont, there is nothing to worry about. Rabies is transmitted by the bite of the infected animal, and the virus, once the animal dies, has a life expectancy of only a few days. If the animal is freshly dead and if you have an open wound on your hand, there is a chance that you might get infected when picking it up. We assume, however, that when you say "skull," you mean the bony remains of the head of something that has been dead long enough that flesh, tissue and fur have disappeared through the process of decomposition. Any trace of rabies virus will be long gone, and you can handle the skull with absolute safety.

Monk's Cave

Q: Years ago while living in western Massachusetts I discovered what I believe to be an unexamined "monk's cave," as they were known then. I had seen monk's caves, in other locations, all of which were dug out or excavated. These caves were holes or hideaways dug into the sides of hills, with a narrow entranceway leading to a small chamber underground. The entranceway and chamber were usually lined with round stones. They were thought to be centuries old, and no one at the time (1960s) knew just who made them. Several are known to exist throughout New England. I do know that the University of Massachusetts at Amherst was investigating them in the mid-1960s.

Getting to the point: I know the location of one such cave, or at least I believe it's one. With development the way it is these days, I feel I should reveal its location to those who might like to study it. As I said it is untouched, full to the top with rotted leaves and soil. It's located deep in the woods, in Massachusetts, near the Vermont border. Who might I call to report its location? I have always intended to return to dig the cave myself, for the artifacts I might find, but have thought better of such a selfish act. Please advise.

J. M. P., Montpelier

A: Giovanna Peebles, the Vermont state archeologist, especially asked us to thank you for not having excavated the cave. She said many potentially valuable archeological sites are destroyed by people who are not professionally trained archeologists, and dig, as you first intended to do, for "artifacts."

Now, as to your "monk's cave," (also know as monk's mounds,

Celtic caves, stone chambers, Indian ceremonial caves and 18th-
and 19th-century root cellars), there is no consensus on what they
actually are or what they were used for, although a majority of
archeologists favor the root-cellar explanation. No matter what
their origin, the caves are considered to be important archeological sites, and you might want to notify the Massachusetts state
archeologist at the Massachusetts Historical Commission in Boston. The organization in New England that is most interested in
the identification, protection and research on these caves or chambers, however, is the New England Antiquities Research Association (NEARA). The person to notify is Betty Peterson, 14 Black
Hill Rd., Paxton, MA 01612.

PITTED GRAVESTONE

Q: My mother's gravestone (it's over 60 years old) is in a cemetery
beside the Connecticut River in the Northeast Kingdom and has
within the past few years become badly pitted by acid rain, as have
almost all others in the cemetery. If it is not treated and preserved,
I fear the inscription will soon disappear. What can I use to clean
it, and what can I use to treat it after cleaning to prevent further
deterioration?

Paul Buzzell, Manchester Center

A: We wish we knew what kind of stone was used for your mother's
monument. We called the Barre Granite Association, and the gent
we spoke to felt certain it wasn't granite, as acid rain isn't hurting
granite. He thought it was probably made of a softer stone such as
marble or sandstone. He said the stone of choice depended on the
area. We asked if there were any marble quarries in the Northeast
Kingdom, and he didn't know of any. We also spoke to Philip at
Gawet Marble and Granite Co. in Rutland. He said that the stone
was probably white marble, which is easier than granite to cut and
sculpt and was very popular 60 years ago. He explained that marble oxidizes, that is, breaks down, as a result of exposure to acid
rain and weather. He said the more highly polished the marble
was, the less moisture it absorbs and the longer it would last. He
suggested you clean the stone with a product called 600 Sure

Clean, which is 1-percent acid. Take a soft brush, like one used to finish sheetrock, dilute the cleaner according to the directions and spread it on the monument. Then rinse the monument and your hands thoroughly. He said a sealer wouldn't be effective unless the marble was highly polished. He also suggested another cleaner that is acid-free called Super-Shine-All, but he thought you would have better luck with the Sure Clean. These products are available at Gawet's and probably from other monument manufacturers. Philip also said that you could take the piece and have it reworked, but that would be expensive.

DANGER IN COBALT-BLUE BOTTLES?

Q: Someone told me that the cobalt-blue bottles I've collected are radioactive. Is that why we see fewer products packaged in them? I've never read any warnings about keeping the bottles around.
Louise Silloway, Randolph Center

A: Don't worry about your cobalt-blue bottles. They are not in the least bit radioactive. The reason you see fewer around is not because they are dangerous, but because the cobalt used in dying the glass is extremely expensive.

BIRD WATCHING

Q: In Putnam County, some 60 miles north of New York City, where we lived until we moved to Vermont last June, weather and specifically winter weather conditions didn't seem so markedly different from what they are here. We would compare observations with our Vermont daughter, and yes, it got colder and often stayed cold longer in Vermont, and true, the snow generally was deeper, but the difference was not radical. Now it's winter, and we've noticed a sharp drop in bird population. The finches, both gold and purple, have disappeared. Nothing has approached our thistle feeder in weeks, perhaps months, whereas in Putnam we always knew finches were there if only because snow under the feeder would be black with spilled seeds. We don't have any of those slate-colored juncos here either. In fact our currently visible bird population appears limited to a cardinal (with offspring), blue jays, nuthatches, chickadees and an occasional (rarely seen) woodpecker. And what about sparrows? We had hardly any of those even in warmer months.

W. F. B., Chester

A: Our source, Sarah Laughlin, director of the Vermont Institute of Natural Sciences and an authority on Vermont birds, said you actually have a pretty good cross section of wintering birds for Vermont woodland. There are many minihabitats in Vermont— hilltops and valleys, for instance—and each will have very different populations of birds. Tree sparrows and juncos are valley winterers, and you will rarely find sparrows of any kind in heavily wooded areas. Siskins and goldfinches are erratic in their appearance from year to year: sometimes there will be lots of them, sometimes none. Sarah also pointed out that much of the thistle seed one buys nowadays has been sterilized because people were worried that fertile seed would turn their lawn into a thistle jungle come summer. The birds just don't like the sterile seed. Not only is it less tasty, but the sterilization process damages the seed's nutritional content.

Sarah advises that if you hang out suet, you will probably have more than just an occasional woodpecker, and if you feed a mixture that contains cracked corn, you may attract mourning doves as well.

The farther north you get, the fewer species of birds you'll come up with. The Vermont Winter Bird Count came up with 35 species of birds in the Woodstock area this year and felt that was doing pretty well; in Massachusetts a bird count in any given area will usually turn up more than 50 different species.

PRESERVING A NEWS CLIPPING

Q: I am in the process of putting together a scrapbook and would like to preserve some newspaper clippings for the book. Is there any way to keep the newspaper from turning yellow and brittle?

Anne, Rutland

A: The acid in newsprint causes the paper to turn yellow and brittle. Here's a concoction which removes the acidity from the paper. Dissolve a milk-of-magnesia tablet in a quart of club soda overnight. Pour into a pan large enough to accommodate the flattened clipping. Paper is fragile when it's wet, so to prevent it from tearing, put a piece of nylon net in the pan beneath the clipping. Soak the clipping for up to one hour. Remove carefully and pat dry. Do not move until paper is completely dry. Place a weight on top of the clipping once it's semidry to prevent its ends from curling.

COMIC-BOOK PRESERVATION

Q: Recently you answered a question about cleaning a refrigerator. Moving one step forward, once the refrigerator is clean, would it be safe to use it as a storage place for comic books, strips and other related comic-art items? I'm perfectly serious in asking this question, as I read that one of the safest places to store comics is in the refrigerator to keep them in mint condition and undamaged by temperature changes, sunlight, etc. As you know, comics are particularly susceptible to the ravages of time due to the acidity of their pulp-paper pages.

T. F., Rutland

A: We assume you are talking about a refrigerator that isn't used for food storage. As you will see from what follows, storing printed matter in a refrigerator also used for food would not be a good idea, as the door would be opened and closed too frequently to keep the temperature stable. If you have an extra refrigerator, however, and don't mind paying the electricity bill, Kim Cosgrove at the New England Document Center, Andover, MA 01810 (617-470-1010), told us a refrigerator is, indeed, a great place to keep comic books, and for exactly the reasons you mentioned. Light, and frequent changes in humidity and temperature are the most important factors to consider in the preservation of any document, comics included. Light will cause the inks to fade and paper to deteriorate. Changes in humidity, which cause the fibers in the paper to expand and contract, speed the process. The ideal temperature for preserving your comics is 68 degrees or lower, with no fluctuation. Kim suggests you put a thermometer in your refrigerator and test for constant temperature maintenance before you put in the comic books. To test the humidity, which should be at 50 percent with no more than a 5-percent fluctuation, you can purchase an hygrometer from any scientific-instrument company or, better yet, ask your local high school if you can borrow one for a few days from their science lab. Good luck.

DEPRESSION GARDENS

Q: Can you give me a recipe for making a Depression garden? I remember my grandmother making them for us when I was a little girl, and now that I have grandchildren, I'd like to do the same for them.

H. P., Proctor

A: Recipe 1: Place three or four pieces of any kind of coal or coke in an open glass dish. (If using charcoal, add a few extra pieces.) Pour 2 tablespoons each of water, liquid bluing and common table salt over the coal. (Add separately.) Let stand 24 hours. Then add 2 more tablespoons of salt. On the third day add 2 tablespoons of liquid ammonia to give a fluffy appearance. The chemical reaction will create a beautiful bowl of flowers—or coral, depending how you look at it!

Recipe 2: Place broken pieces of brick or terra cotta clay in a glass bowl or jar. Pour the following solution over this: 4 teaspoons water, 1 teaspoon ammonia, 4 teaspoons bluing, 1 teaspoon Mercurochrome, 4 teaspoons salt. Add more of this solution each day until the crystal garden has grown to desired size.

RUBBER GLOVES: REPAIRS AND REMARKS

Q: I have to keep my hands out of water because of a problem a lot of people (men and women) have—"housewife's eczema." I use rubber gloves to do the dishes and other cleaning and am always getting a little pinhole in one of them, which makes the pair totally useless. I have been throwing them out but was wondering if you have any ideas on how to repair them. I am a fairly young house-wife with a lot of years left to waste rubber gloves. I would appreci-ate any suggestions.

M., Barre

A: We called the Development Department of Goodyear Rubber, in Windsor (Goodyear has since closed its branch there), as we had always heard that the best rubber chemists came from Windsor, Vermont. The chemist we spoke with explored various options with us and concluded none of them were liability-free. He sug-gested you write to the manufacturer of the gloves and ask if there is a product available for rubber repair that would work on their gloves.

READER FEEDBACK: We received a veritable flood of mail on this question: here's a sampling.

Frank Teagle, of Woodstock, wrote: "No Windsor rubber chem-ist I, but 13 years experience in handling broken glass at our late-lamented Re-Du Center wearing heavy-duty rubber-impregnated canvas gloves taught me a lot about their repair.

"M. in Barre should be able to get lots more wear out of pin-holed gloves very easily. All she needs is a tube of Devcon Rubber Mender, available at any hardware store. Lightweight rubber from 5/8-inch rubber bands cut into little patches should work fine, and she can scrounge the rubber bands from any postmaster! Or, since it's just water she wants to keep out, she can sacrifice one of her old gloves to be used for patching material.

"Method of mending: locate the pinhole by blowing up the glove like a balloon and plunging it into a basin of water and watching for bubbles. Circle these areas with a waterproof felt-tipped marker. Dry surfaces inside and out and cut small patches to fit the marked area. Apply a thin coat of Devcon to both glove and one side of the patch and let dry a few minutes. Then press the two coated surfaces firmly together. The patch will stick like an attic window, instantly!

"Not recommended for brain surgeons, but fine for dish-washers."

Shirley Gage, of Rochester, wrote: "There is a product called Kiwi Sport and Shoe Patch that will mend rubber gloves: it won't last forever but will help."

Margaret Audette, of Springfield, wrote: "I wish M. in Barre would read Adele Davis' *Let's Get Well* and *Let's Eat Right to Get Fit* so she would take yeast and use E-, C-, and B-vitamins and cure the eczema. Rubber gloves make it worse. I have been through this myself and also work in nutrition, so speak knowledgeably."

PLAYING CARDS THAT STICK TOGETHER

Q: I have a brand-new set of playing cards that are very expensive. They stick together, and they're really useless this way. Can you tell me how to unstick them?

Unsigned, Poultney

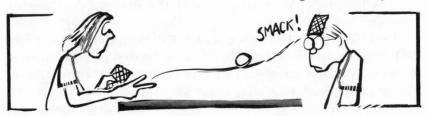

A: We didn't know the answer, but our mailbox bulged with letters from people who had suggestions galore.

Vinnie Pena, of Barre, said to wax the backs of the cards with Simonize car wax and rub with a soft cloth. "This works wonders," she wrote.

Many wrote to say that dusting the playing cards with talcum powder, cornstarch or cornmeal will do the trick. Several ways of applying the above were suggested. Julie Follet, of Whiting, grew up in Panama, where the humidity is high. "Before shuffling the deck, we'd thumb through the cards while sprinkling a little talcum powder through." Frank T., of Woodstock, suggests: "Sprinkle and spread talcum powder on a smooth, flat surface. Place cards face down and slide gently around on the powder. Tap off excess and reconstitute the pack so the powder on the face of one card will transfer and coat the back side of another. Tapping the pack several times on a hard surface and a good shuffling will make them slide easily again."

Several readers suggested putting the cards in a bag with powder, cornstarch or cornmeal and shaking them around.

ARMY RECORDS

Q: I have become interested in writing an account of my World War II experiences and thought that my children and grandchildren might find them to be of interest as well. As a means of assuring the accuracy of such an account, I would be greatly benefited by access to my service record. I have been told that the depository for records of the army is located in the St. Louis area, but I have been unable to learn its address. Perhaps your sources would be more productive.

A. H., Bellows Falls

A: You need to obtain Form 180 from the Veterans Administration. In Vermont you can do this by calling the VA Assistance and Information Office at 802-295-2582 or writing the Veterans Administration, North Hartland Rd, White River Junction, VT 05001. It would be a good idea to write "Request for Form" on the lower-left-hand corner of the envelope. You can then fill out the form and mail it to: United States Army, Bureau of Documents, 97 Page Blvd., St. Louis, MO 63132.

INDEX